Praise for
Teaching From The Inside Out

So light and inviting – it really makes one want to try it out. The writing is clear and straightforward and friendly. The concrete experiences are especially rich and suggestive.
Stephan Fredman
Professor of English and the Joseph Morahan Director
of Core Courses, University of Notre Dame

I like your text very much. It feels like you have taken an injured and bewildered teacher in, and under your kind and empowering guidance, showed them another way – a more natural and less strenuous way – to shift their role from being a teacher to being an educator. I think you are absolutely correct in this, and your clear and enthusiastic tone is wise and reassuring... The style of your writing fits so well the point you are making – it's okay to be yourself! It's okay to start from the immediacy of our current situation. It's what artists – of all disciplines – do. Why not teachers too? The authenticity of your work is affirmed by the personal stories you tell of your own efforts. I think this is most valuable, especially for educators who have been cajoled endlessly to be fearless and creative, but offered no model of what that may actually look and feel like in the classroom setting. I think [this book] is solid and necessary reading.
Peter London
Author of *No More Second Hand Art: Awakening
The Artist Within*
Professor Art Education,
Southeastern Massachusetts University

This book is a celebration of the joy of teaching.
Marie Schilling
Fourth Grade Teacher
William H. Ray Elementary School, Chicago

Sue Sommers shows brilliantly again and again how following what you love leads to effective action-in-the-world. Her book is inspiring, experience-based, full of insights into what teaching and learning are about. Teaching From The Inside Out *will raise your energy level, awaken your creativity, and generate untold numbers of new ideas for the classroom. A wonderful contribution to our knowledge and education. And [this is] not just for teachers – this book is for everybody. It's marvelous.*

Jane Tompkins, Ph.D.
Author of *A Life in School: What the Teacher Learned*

Her voice – quiet and thoughtful, yet bright and energetic too – speaks with warm familiarity. Her book is a good friend with whom I can reminisce about experiences that are old, new, funny, bewildering, frustrating, magical and memorable. It helps me find that lost favorite thing that sparks my artfulness and lets me shine in my world. This book is a friend to dialogue with, someone to ask how to and then find ways that are not spelled out as answers, but rather as "Practices" to try out. Sue Sommers speaks with sensitivity, clarity, and purpose.

Mary Acierto Ridley
Visual Art Teacher, Nettlehorst School, Chicago

An empowering book on using the arts as an inspirational teaching tool as well as a means for personal growth. With creative approaches to learning the key to cultivating a more interactive classroom, visual artist Sue Sommers leads the reader through a journey of discovery of one's own artistic gifts. She shares valuable exercercises and personal experiences and suggests methods to help teachers overcome stumbling blocks.

Tim Sauers
Director of Programs, Urban Gateways
The Center for Arts in Education, Chicago

With a rare mix of good sense, humor, imagination and practicality, Teaching From The Inside Out *proposes a different way of thinking, teaching and learning, which is very resourceful and inspiring. Sue Sommer's unique approach to teaching links the creative process and art to deep spiritual values and to her belief in the essential beauty and goodness of all beings. At the same time, Sue reveals a great sensitivity for and understanding of the challenges and demands teachers face today, and she offers them her very wise and useful eight-fold path – a guide toward creativity rather than conformity. There is a freshness and enthusiasm in* Teaching From The Inside Out *that will warm the heart of every devoted teacher and which has the potential to engender more wisdom and joy in our educational institutions. This is a book well worth reading.*

Marlene De Nardo
Director of Naropa University Master of Liberal Arts
Program in Creation Spirituality, Oakland, CA

Artists and educators have always held a kinship, as each artist is a teacher, and each teacher an artist. Sue Sommers has composed a brilliant score to act as a blueprint for teachers, artist collaborators, and facilitators. Teaching From The Inside Out *is not simply an integral tool for the educator and artist, but a groundbreaking guide for living an artful life.*

David Miller, Muscian and Educator
Founder Orchestra X and Evanston Music Academy

...an eloquent and moving account of an artist/teacher who has worked directly with children and teachers as a facilitator. Sommers describes a "fluid process" that enables self-discovery and realization. She references her own experience as an artist and from there moves to ways that these same insights inform our teaching.

Jerome J. Hausman, Ph.D.
Visiting Professor, School of the Art Institute, Chicago
Former President, Minneapolis College of Art & Design

Reunion 2000

For Lynn + fly Alan . . .
Longtime good friends
there thick + thin, You are
good friends to have in both —
Much Love,
Susie

TEACHING FROM
THE INSIDE OUT

The Eight-fold Path to
Creative Teaching (and Living)

Sue Sommers 2000

by Sue Sommers

with a Foreword by
William Ayers

Authority Press Inc.

Printed in the United States of America.

03   02   01   00   1   2   3   4

Library of Congress Cataloging-in-Publication Data
Sommers, Sue, 1933-
   Teaching from the inside out: the eight-fold path to creative teaching (and living) / by Sue Sommers with a foreward by William Ayers.

      p.cm.
   ISBN 1-929059-02-7
   1. Creative thinking–Study and teaching (Elementary) 2. Elementary school teaching. 3. Art–Study and teaching (Elementary) I. Title.
   LB1590.5.S65 2000
   372.13–dc21

                        00-009210

Authority Press Inc.
10970 Morton's Crossing
Alpharetta, GA 30022
770-475-2837
www.authoritypress.com

Publisher: Eric E. Torrey
Cover Design: Craig Hall, Streambed Graphics
Cover Art: Created by 8th grade students at
                  Seward School in Chicago
Printer: Sheridan Books

TEACHING FROM THE INSIDE OUT

The Eight-fold Path to Creative Teaching (and Living)

by Sue Sommers

with a Foreword by
William Ayers

To teachers everywhere,
in and out of the classroom

and

For my most memorable teachers
who have taught me some of my most valuable lessons:
my parents – Dorothy and Milton Jacoby
my first mentor – Mabel Johnson
my spiritual teachers – Dorothy Day,
Baba Maktananda, and Elihu Smith
my husband – Tor
my children – Stephanie, Marc, Cecily, and Chris

CONTENTS

Foreword

Here is a lovely book by a working artist about a quality
all good teachers cultivate: artfulness. Teaching From The
Inside Out is not directly about painting or sculpture or
dance; neither is it a text on art in the schools. Sue
Sommers focuses our attention, rather, on the path we all
must travel—indeed the path we are traveling—from
inexperienced to experienced, from clumsy to skilled, from
innocent to wise. Because she respects both the walker
and the way, Sommers demonstrates again and again that
artfulness is entirely accessible—never the exclusive
province of the gifted or the chosen—and that with some
thought and some effort we can learn to make artfulness
a defining quality in our classrooms.

Teaching is often a mysterious enterprise, a paradoxi-
cal activity. There are, of course, bodies of knowledge to
somehow convey—an exponentially increasing cargo in
our rapidly expanding universe—and yet we all know that
knowledge will lie flat upon the floor, inert and as dead as
a door nail, disconnected from the living minds of learners
unless we tap into the deeply human qualities of curiosity,
desire, the delight in being able to do and to know.
Teachers are expected to transmit or disseminate the
goods, so to speak, and yet we also know that teachers
must find a way to see their students as full human
beings with hopes and dreams, skills and capacities, interests and concerns that must somehow be addressed if
learning is to occur. Teachers must discover a path toward
reversal—becoming students of their students in order for
the project of learning and teaching to become robust and
powerful and energizing. Embracing the mystery of teach-

ing, living with complexity and inconsistency and contradiction, is an important part of becoming an artful teacher.

The artful teacher is attentive and aware. She or he strives to see more and hear more in order to understand more. She is wide-awake. She practices noticing and listening—the disciplines of artfulness. She also takes care of herself, her mind and heart and soul.

This posture in the world allows the teacher to rise to the intellectual and ethical challenges of teaching. She sees her responsibility, then, as attending to the life and learning of this child, and then this one, and then this—each the one and only who will ever trod the earth. She understands that what she holds in her hands is precious, not to be taken-for-granted, diminished or broken. She takes responsibility, too, for constructing an environment that is deep enough and wide enough to nourish and challenge the wide range of students who enter her classroom. She is alert for the teachable moments that present themselves in the everyday, and ready to ask what knowledge and experiences are of most value in this intensely dynamic community of learners. She is a teacher who cares about the world enough to worry about its future and her students place in it; and she cares about her students enough to provide them the tools and dispositions that will enable full participation in a world they themselves will help construct. She cares, as well, about herself, about nourishing herself at her own adult level, and so she reads and writes and attends plays and makes art herself.

We live, of course, in a world in many ways out of balance, a world in need of repair. Childhood itself is precarious for many. Some of our children are dying needlessly, others are living brutish lives of hopelessness and despair. They don't know where to turn. Teachers should be in the front-line saying with passion and conviction that they can turn to us. Artful teachers show us how this can be done. Turn to us.

William Ayers
Distinguished Professor
College of Education
University of Illinois at Chicago
Author of *A Kind and Just Parent*

ACKNOWLEDGEMENTS

I don't believe that any of us does anything alone. That is certainly true of the book you hold in your hands.

This book came into being as a result of my frustration going in and out of the Chicago public schools as I worked with teachers and children around using the arts in the curriculum. I felt saddened that they had to leave themselves out of enjoying the process of always creating something new out of themselves. So I wrote this book as a way of talking to and thanking all the wonderful teachers whom I have had contact with, too numerous to mention individually. They especially inspired me.

I am indebted to fellow artist and educator, Bonnie Hartenstein, for her stimulating converstations and ideas as this project began. Her insights were a great contribution.

I have also been inspired by friends, colleagues and valued fellow artists who share the same concerns I do about art and education. Through their words and ideas, but mostly through their being, they have added to the writing of this book: Charity James, Shirley Gunther, Ronne Hartfield, Jerry Hausman, M.C. Richards, and Dan Scheinfeld.

I did my best to incorporate the countless suggestions from those who read this in manuscript form and encouraged me at different times in its birthing process: Bill Ayers, Meg Barden, Suzanne Cohan-Lange, Nancy Cusack, Shirley Rounds Davis, Marlene DeNardo, Stephen and Katherine Fredman, Ruth Felton, Matthew Fox, Cynthia Gehrie, Peggy Jacoby, Peter London, Eileen and Doug McClatchy, Jean Parisi, Marge Roche, Kayla

Russick, Marie Schilling, Sue Shellenbarger, Elihu Smith, Alain Van Kirk, and Lynn White.

CACT, the Chicago Arts Collaborative for Teachers, has been a singular inspiration in the arts and education field. Its philosophy of experiencial learning has helped inform my thoughts about what it means to be an arts facilitator. I am grateful to the collaborative model of learning and teaching and to the other artists and administrators I have had the pleasure of working with: Karl Androes, Brigid Finucane, Drea Howenstein, Little Tom Jackson, Marva Jolly, Cathy Larsen, Lauri Macklin, David Miller, Barbara Pawlikowski, Richard Pettingill, Avo Randruut, Nana Shineflug, Rodney Stapleton, and Bobbi Stuart. It's been a great team! And thank you to Scott Nobey-Brandon and the Lincoln Center Institute for their clear approach to incorporating an artistic approach to teaching.

Thanks to other inspiring artist educators: Suzanna Aguilar, Glenda Baker, Elizabeth Johnston, Emily Hooper, Kathleen Maltese, Donna Mandel, Laura Sollman St. John, and Cynthia Weiss. Each, in their individual way, taught me more about this important work.

Thanks to my editor, Marcia Broucek, who guided me through this work. I am also grateful to Eric E. Torrey, publisher at Authority Press, whose enthusiasm for this project has helped maintain my own.

I thank my husband, Tor Faegre, who has cheered me on throughout.

INTRODUCTION

I was getting ready to leave a fourth grade classroom in one of Chicago's overcrowded inner city schools. It was 2:00 P.M., a half hour before school let out. I had been doing a residency in that room earlier in the day and had returned to collect my coat. It had just begun to thunder outside and the rumbling cracks held everyone spellbound—except the teacher. She heard it. Everyone did. That thunder simply revealed its presence unmistakably.

"Notice me," it seemed to say.

The teacher, noting the clock, said, "Ahh, we'll do some poetry for the last half hour. Come to the rug, children."

They came and she reviewed the seasons, all four of them—one at a time. All the while the thunder was roaring. The children were trying to be obedient and pay attention to the lesson, but they were "oooing" and "ahhhing" and being scared by the sudden intrusions of loud rolls of thunder.

"Fall, that's where we were," the teacher persisted. "Eric, pay attention. What happens in the fall?"

The children spoke up and out came their stored knowledge, unconnected from their interests and feelings.

"What shall we write about," she questioned.

At that moment, I blurted out, "Why not write about the thunder?"

She didn't notice. She seemed determined to continue with her lesson. I left the classroom, heartsick at this lost opportunity. Here was nature being insistent and only the children were listening. The teacher could have made space in her "plan" by noticing the storm and asking the

xvii

children to investigate it. She might then have asked them what thunder sounded like and how it made them feel. Then they could have have written poetry. That would have been artful teaching.

An artist pays attention to her surroundings. All of us can become artists and be aware of and in tune with the world's rhythms. The world creates and destroys itself all the time. To understand that, all we have to do is look around us.

The crocuses just bloomed their first tiny "hello" the other day. There they were in all their new glory, translucent purples and yellows opening up to the hopeful spring-like warmth in early March. Then, abruptly the weather turned cold and—ZAP—all that was gone. When I went out into my neighbors' yard to look at the new flowers, to look closely into their faces, into the fragile heart of their first flowering, I felt so hopeful. I grabbed my drawing board and watercolors in order to catch their glory on paper so I could experience the openness in my heart that they had inspired. When I opened the door I was met with a blast of cold air; the temperature had dipped thirty degrees in the ten minutes I was gathering my art supplies. It was too cold and too windy to sit outside—and too cold for the purple and yellow petals to stand this sudden shift in temperature. That night it snowed and when I dug out a fragile crocus the next day, it was closed and had fallen over like it was bowing to the elements, simply giving itself to this unexpected winter storm. As I looked at it, I was struck with the surrender with which it responded to the elements. That we could all open and close so gracefully!

Taken together, these stories come from my experience as an artist-facilitator in the public schools and also as a working artist. The first story, and others like it, need to be told because they expand our concept of how school environments frustrate teachers and burden them with excessive demands. Daily expectations rob teachers of the energy and interest necessary for personal expression and the creative solutions needed for the demanding task of how and when to teach what. Teachers and their students face sterilized robot-like school days if they don't pay attention. They miss the crocuses blooming outside and inside themselves and lose their greatest resource—their own interests. When personal interests are encouraged to become a source of creative imagining about how and what to teach, teachers naturally discover enthusiasm for their work, which then translates into the classroom, energizing and empowering the students. Examples from my own and others' experience narrate the many forms that creativity can take to produce lively classrooms where both teachers and children are inspired and challenged. The stories demonstrate how using artistic approaches to learning can support self-expression, self-discipline, and alert observations on the world around us as well as to inspire confidence in one's own source and power of creativity.

The first chapter proposes that what we love gives us energy to explore our interests. I chronicle experiences in numerous schools and how alien these environments are to searching for and teaching from our own interests. We look at ingrained habits, both inside ourselves—our own fears—and the reality of the educational system as I have encountered it, that keep us from exploration.

In the second chapter I explore how to take simple mundane situations and turn them into curriculum. Acknowledging our interests produces confidence and allows us to make the necessary correlation between our lives inside and outside of our work situations. We see that this is the way artists work and that we all have potential to become artists at what we do.

The third chapter begins by looking at a remarkable teacher, Sylvia Ashton-Warner, author of *Teacher*—who cultivated attitudes in a difficult teaching situation (she was a New Zealander teaching Maori Indians) allowing her to turn her classroom into a vibrant learning environment. Having analyzed what she did, I present eight attitudes that must be present if a teacher is to manifest creativity in the classroom. Practicing these attitudes as essential ingredients for artful teaching, teachers might find themselves opening up to a whole new world of teaching.

In the fourth chapter I tell stories from the moments I have had as an artist-facilitator in three different teaching situations. These varied experiences in classrooms illuminate the process of honoring our interests, going beyond our blocks, staying in the confusion and emerging from a creative learning experience with knowledge and self-esteem.

At the end of each chapter there are a series of reflections, culled from the material, which are concrete practices for maximizing and maintaining creativity. They are in the form of questions which help to uncover a person's felt interests and the blocks that prevent creativity from being a natural part of the daily classroom. They are intended to create a structure in which old habits can be challenged while allowing more authentic beliefs to emerge.

I have written a short appendix specifically about art facilitation, a term I use to describe the process needed for artists to impact schools. I chronicle a specific way of training artists to work with teachers. I hope that other artists and art educators who wish to impact education will find encouragement and direction from this section.

In all, this book is about artful teaching. It attempts to heal the split between theory and practice. It isn't a recipe book, nor is it a theoretical tract. Instead it is informed by experience and has its roots in the ancient belief in humanism and the arts.

Although the audience for this book could be anyone interested in becoming more creative, it is addressed primarily to people who are concerned with learning. And because what impacts teachers should have broad appeal, this book is for others concerned with schools also—university professors of education, principals, administrators, other artist-facilitators, arts and education organizations, policy makers, researchers, as well as parents concerned with how teachers influence children. I hope that this will be both inspirational as well as practical.

I know that teachers are overworked and underpaid and that they are asked to do the impossible. I do not want to add to their burden, but simply to help in finding a way of reorganizing an already too-full plate. Reading a book won't make you a different person, but it might help you explore different ways of thinking. Practicing makes a difference, and if we practice noticing, we don't miss the loud thunderstorms or the subtle crocuses opening and closing.

Teachers need more support if they are going to make a difference for our children. Over the years, I have come to honor them and the overwhelming challenge of being a teacher. I have come to respect their efforts to teach despite pressures from all sides—principals, administrators, parents, and the children themselves. In both public and private schools, I have encountered the most talented teachers constrained by bureaucratic burdens, and emerging teachers soured by mountains of paperwork. My goal has been to inspire teachers to be creative, to honor their interests and thereby to form a personal teaching style around their strengths. Admittedly, there is so much pressure to conform, to excel by using children's reading and math scores as yardsticks of their teaching ability. This leaves little time—and certainly lends no support—for roaming around in one's personal experiences in order to bring a different attitude to the classroom. Creativity is usually marginalized and trivialized. School cultures breed a lifeless conformity instead of an energetic quest after a genuine experience and the knowledge that it produces. Over-disciplining children, enforcing them to learn what someone else thinks important, learning by rote or intimidation, allowing screeching sounds (euphemistically called "bells") to pierce the day's activities—all of these things create an atmosphere of combat, and everyone in this kind of system suffers.

I believe that exploration and reflection ought to be encouraged and made the center for an education of meaning. There is tremendous value in knowing what inspires us. Might our own interests become the means for our continued deepening? Might we trust that they are relevant to learning and the core from which we can create an inspired curriculum? Might the arts help us in this search?

We could reflect on these questions. We can't sit by and watch the children suffer. Political changes make some difference. Financial help buys materials. It is also an incentive to teachers. But the real change needs to come in the classroom itself. Whatever else is done, it isn't enough if what happens in the classroom doesn't change qualitatively.

Administrators might ask themselves these kinds of far-reaching questions, so that any change in policy on the administrative level is sensitive to the real needs of children, not simply a palliative for improving test scores; and to the real needs of teachers to whom we entrust our children. I hope that administrators will be interested in this approach to education.

No matter what, this is a call for teachers to take back their inner power and to facilitate children's development as if the nation's life depended on it.

It does.

NOTE

This book is demanding and I realize that anyone wanting quick fixes to difficult problems may be disappointed. I couldn't write a book in which we might all share the same delusion that recipes for creative teaching will work. What I have written instead is about our own work on ourselves, work that I believe might facilitate the changes that our schools need. This book invites you to take a journey. It's a difficult though useful journey, and utlimately, the only one worth taking.

BEFORE YOU BEGIN

Take some time to read and ponder the following paragraph. Write down your responses and store them in a safe place so you can come back to them after you have finished reading this book. At that time, you will be asked to repeat the same exercise and compare it with what you wrote at the outset to see if your goal has changed.

> Focus on your main goal in being an educator, the one that is your driving force. (Do not let others' expectations intrude.) Write it large in a simple sentence. Contemplate what your teaching would look like to make that goal a reality and write down your description.

*"In many schools, teaching is expected to follow syllabi
that lay out what students will learn, as well as
when and how they will learn it. But in a real classroom,
whether kindergarten, graduate school, or the school of
life, there are live people with personal needs and
knowledge. A particular tap in this direction will shift this
person's perspective; after today's discussion you know
that this reading will be good to assign, based on what
seems like the natural flow to the next step. You cannot
plan these things. You have to teach each person, each
class group, and each moment as a particular case that
calls out for particular handling. Planning an agenda of
learning without knowing who is going to be there, what
their strengths and weaknesses are, how they interact,
prevents surprises and prevents learning. The teacher's art
is to connect, in real time, the living bodies of the students
with the living body of the knowledge."*

Stephen Nachmanovitch
FREE PLAY
Improvisation in Life and Art
(pp. 20)

Starting With Your Own Energy

"You Don't Have to Drink Your Tomato Juice"

When I walk into classrooms, I often find teachers presenting curriculum to disengaged students. Discipline problems arise that the teacher needs to control in order to continue imparting the information that bores her and her students. Yet, there is a sense that everyone is doing what they are supposed to be doing. This pervasive educational situation reminds me of a story I have always loved, told by the great teacher and mythologist Joseph Campbell.

While he was in a restaurant one evening having dinner, he overheard a conversation at a nearby table:

1

"Drink your tomato juice," a father instructed his twelve-year-old son.

"But," protested the child, "I don't like tomato juice."

"Drink it anyway," insisted the father.

The child's mother came to her son's rescue and insisted to her husband that the child shouldn't have to drink his tomato juice if he didn't want to.

Whereupon the father said in anguish, "I've never done a thing I wanted to do in all my life."

With sad humor, this story sums up the horror of living a life for everyone but oneself. Following other people's values destroys what is truly real in us and focuses us on whatever we think others want us to be like, such as what might give us status or material gain. Asking ourselves if our clothes have the right labels, if our cars are jazzy enough, or if the books that we read or the friends that we have make us worth knowing is like always drinking our tomato juice, even when we do not like it.

Campbell's own life exemplified not drinking his tomato juice. He did what he truly wanted, what he called "following your bliss." When he was offered an opportunity to compile an anthology of myths, he refused. Instead, he risked a promising start early in his career by choosing to do what he felt he needed to do: spend time alone reading and reflecting.

What might happen if we did what we liked, explored our fantasies, acted upon our interests? Who would we be? What kinds of lives would we live? What kinds of parents, artists, or business people would we be? What kinds of teachers would we become? And what might our children learn about how to be themselves?

A friend of mine who teaches art told me she was going to have the children in one of her classes select a favorite interest and make an art project from it. Then she waved her hands in the air, creating a grand sweeping generality, saying, "And I will teach the world view." Puzzled and wanting to be specific, I inquired what she liked to do, what her interests were.

She sighed and said, "I'm so busy, I can't think about what I'd like to do for at least another year and a half!"

"Just think of one thing that you really like to do," I pleaded. She became reflective for a moment and then a smile began to creep up the corners of her mouth.

"You know," she said almost conspiratorially, "I love to make salads." Her body posture began to change as she continued. "I'm interested in feeding myself well, and I love to create beautiful and nutritious salads—perhaps put in kiwi fruit—they're so wonderful."

Contemplating her sudden enthusiasm for salads, I asked, "Why couldn't you develop a whole curriculum around salad? You could, with the kids, create salads with all kinds of fruits and vegetables. The kids could get into their favorite foods. You could even grow a garden—inside or out. Just think what you could learn about nutrition as you studied it. And about horticulture as you watched things grow. And color and composition. Salads could be the basis for studying painting. You might even create salad sculptures from clay. And what about studying salads of other lands? It's all there."

We bantered back and forth for a while as both of us became more and more delighted about the array of possibilities. As teachers, couldn't we saturate our curricula with our own enthusiasm by focusing on our own interests? We could begin with any interest, no matter how small or insignificant it seems to us, and generate material for as long as we wish.

3

William Blake said we can learn "to see the world in a grain of sand . . . " This is true—if we find the grain of sand we are interested in. But what if we don't? We might then ask ourselves, "What prevents us from finding our grain of sand?"

The Blocks: Stumbling or Building

Once upon a time there was a sculptor who made the most beautiful marble elephants. Each one was a masterpiece. Each one had so much life that it seemed as though the trunks were actually swinging while the elephant was sauntering along. People would come to watch the sculptor, and they were invariably in awe as they watched him carve.

"How do you do it?" people would ask him over and over again.

"Oh," he would say, "it's simple, I just chip away at everything that's not the elephant."

What was this sculptor's secret? He seemed to know that the elephant was embedded within the marble and that it was his duty as a sculptor to uncover it. He was the marble's servant, and it was through his surrender to that material that the elephant within was revealed.

What he demonstrated is the universal truth that we are all perfect within, that each of us has an essential inner beauty, a true "us," that is there for the discovery. But too often our identification with who we think we are or ought to be keeps us from seeing our authentic self, our "inner elephant." Second guessing and always trying to be right blinds us to our own beauty and keeps us searching everywhere but inside ourselves to discover it. But, perhaps the biggest stumbling block of all to uncovering our gifts is our fear of the unknown.

4

Fear. We all experience it. It is either a stumbling block or a building block. We are either paralyzed by it or it serves us. When we are paralyzed, our hearts beat fast, we become contracted and defensive. We disassociate. We shut down, no longer hearing ourselves or others. We begin to doubt ourselves, and we justify our fear.

As an artist, I know fear. It happens every time I face a blank canvas, paper, mind, classroom. It is normal. But if we can remember that fear is born of the mind and that the mind is ever-changing, we can experience each little disturbance of fear like a wave in the ocean and know that it will eventually calm down. Fear can give us information: It can tell us that we are afraid to be ourselves, or afraid to take the risks we need to take.

The late Swami Muktananda, a contemporary Indian teacher said, "You shouldn't attach any value to fear because fear is nothing but a movement in the mind."

It helps to understand that. It also helps to know that whenever we try something creative—which means that we are facing something new, never done before by us— that our first instinct is to feel the fear, the anxiety. It can become the signal for us that we are embarking on a creative adventure.

"Oh," we can say to ourselves, "I know you. You are simply telling me that I'm about to take a risk and create something." We can recognize the symptoms and go on. Fear can serve us when we face it. When the stomach turns over and the breath becomes short, we can simply watch it.

Experiment for a moment. Sit down and make yourself comfortable. Put your feet flat on the floor and fold your hands in your lap. Close your eyes and focus your attention on your breath as it comes in and goes out. Just

5

notice how you are breathing; don't try to change it. Keep paying close attention, and whatever feelings emerge, stay with them. Stay with your breath. Don't fight or deny anxiety, tension in your body, or shortness of breath, if that is what is there for you. Don't cling to feelings of calm and contentment, if that is what is there for you. Everything is always changing, and by simply noticing what is there, we can, in time, learn to just see the constantly changing feelings we experience, without comment. Whatever is happening, acknowledge that moment and then take the next breath and be with that. In this way, we can stay open to what is.

Rather than fearing fear and using all our creative energy to deny it, we can make friends with fear by exploring it. Then we have an opportunity to be still and not run from the fear that would run us if we didn't confront it. Rumi, the thirteenth century Persian poet, once said, "Inside you there's an artist you don't know about." Perhaps as we learn to honor our inner artist, rather than fear it, we will be able to carve our own elephants.

Education: The Way It Is

I had been working with a fifth grade teacher and her students on a science and art project for almost a semester. The kids were creating imaginative creatures with clay, stimulated by our study of natural selection. One day as I was wandering around the classroom, looking at the work and noting additions and corrections to the small sculptures that the students were engrossed in, I noticed Leonardo's rapt attention as he was shaping a clearly unique and imaginative piece. Since I like to point out what I see to teachers so they can have another view of their students, I said to this teacher, with great enthusiasm, "Look at Leonardo's sculpture. It's outstanding!"

Her comment: "But he can't read."

I froze and my heart sank, but I managed to continue: "You could use art for this child. It could be a way to engage this child in reading . . ."

As she walked away, I understood that another child who could easily be engaged through the arts was not going to be and that, sadly, his case could be multiplied a million-fold.

It would have helped if this teacher could have been able to acknowledge her own limitations in supporting all the Leonardo's she taught. These kinds of personal fears are one thing, only part of the picture. Working in a situation in which our creativity is thwarted is quite another. Most teachers, like Leonardo's, are captive of what "they" (whoever the "they" happen to be) think students should be taught. No one seems to know better than the "experts" what Jessica and Jimmy should learn. There are endless panels on what ought to be taught, countless curriculum guides on every subject instructing instructors which nouns and verbs should be learned in second grade; how to diagram a sentence; which countries to study in primary, middle, and upper grades, etc. And, as if that were not enough outside pressure, there are endless "mastery" tests to prepare for and administer. By the time the material gets to the children, it is D -E - A - D. The proliferation of teacher materials, curriculum guides—plus the school's expectations for what and when the children should learn—is enough to stagger anyone with even a small measure of sensitivity.

The great danger of this overwhelming and numbing daily life in our schools is that we get further and further away from our own passion. We end up looking every-where but to ourselves for material to teach. We risk los-ing the very center of our own lives which—if explored and valued—could be the source of a dynamic education. And we are robbed of the time to consider the other source of a dynamic education: the creative center of our students' lives.

In virtually all the schools that I have worked in, cre-ativity has not been a high priority. It is not understood and, therefore, not valued. Whatever wisdom national or local commissions are imparting about the importance of the arts in education seems to be falling on deaf ears. Most people in our educational system have not really grasped what the arts could do in the schools: how the arts could unify curriculum, bring enthusiasm to teachers and children, and infuse everyone with a large supply of self-esteem. Too often administrators' primary focus is to bring the reading and math scores up, and the usual plan is to do more of the same: more drill and more tests. The result of this philosophy has not been very effective, judg-ing by the continuing poor test results. The current method of forcing children to learn has not worked yet and, knowing what we do about learning and self-esteem, it does not seem likely that it ever will.

We are all born curious, creative, and spontaneous. This is what allows us to live fully and joyfully—and so often gets crushed out of us as we grow into adults. We leave our delight in the world and become cautious and take life very seriously. How to recapture what we already are—despite the difficulties within us or our environment—is our challenge and our opportunity. Being our spontaneous and authentic selves is our birthright. If we, as adults, can have the courage to discover—no, to uncover—that incredible delight within, the children with whom we work will simply, very naturally unfold their uniquely creative gifts.

The other major problem in education is the discomfort classroom teachers have with the arts. Despite school personnel thinking that the arts are somehow a "good idea," there is massive resistance to being artful in the schools. And because teachers are used to thinking of the arts as separate from the curriculum—another subject like all the rest of the "separate subjects"—they too often do not see how the arts could be used within the curriculum.

I have found to my surprise that this is the situation whether in inner city public schools or private boarding schools. Most of my experience has been in the public schools, but I had entertained the fantasy that private schools would be different. However, while talking to an art teacher in a very prestigious eastern boarding school, I asked her if the classroom teachers there used her to help them with art-related curriculum. "No," she reported, "they are so busy keeping up with their curriculum and feel so much pressure that they have no time for that."

Whether the pressures are to help upper-middle class children into the next stage of competitive schooling or to bring poor inner city children's reading scores up to acceptable standards, the same attitude prevails. Teachers are burdened with too many responsibilities and frozen in old patterns, immersed in an educational atmosphere infected by pervasive seriousness, leaving little room for experimentation, for seeing the situation in new and fresh ways. Teachers need to have more time to fool around, to allow their natural interests to emerge so that they can teach from a totally different perspective.

While this is the reality of the schools in America, we must somehow find our way through this maze of confusion and resistance. Teaching by example is one tonic for dealing with these massive problems. Our children's creative life is at stake.

Education: The Way It Could Be

At one time I worked on a Ford Foundation grant in two Chicago Public Schools as part of a team of seven people devoted to studying the ingredients of teacher development. Each of us had a different role. I was the artist who worked with the teachers in the classrooms by leading activities and by offering workshops. All of us considered ourselves facilitators, people who would do whatever it would take to create an atmosphere in which personal and meaningful learning could take place.

But we did not know how to do what we desperately wanted to do, so we spent a lot of time talking theory to the staff—or waiting for the teachers to ask for our help. We neither acknowledged our particular interests nor tried to find out those of the teachers. There was much caution and little energy. We waited and they waited. Whatever our strategies, they were not working.

One day, I had a brainstorm. I was at the Field Museum in Chicago, standing upstairs by a Tibetan exhibit of papier mache masks, when, suddenly, I knew what I wanted to do. Without hesitation, I took my sketch pad

10

and wrote down "murals, papier mache, puppets." It was that clear. I had never made a mural, but I loved the idea of lots of people working together to generate a common theme, of the community effort involved in carrying that out. I loved folk traditions and the way folk artists made objects from natural materials. I did not know much about papier mache, but I thought that I would love to learn. I was certain that we could make all kinds of wonderful sculptures and masks in that medium. I had done some work with puppets, and I knew that they had great power to help children discover deeper aspects of themselves.

At the very next faculty meeting, I stood up and announced that I wanted to make murals, papier mache sculptures, and puppets and that if anyone else wanted to work with me along those lines, they could let me know. Almost everyone was interested. My enthusiasm for these three art forms seemed to ignite everyone's. It was magic. I was astonished that so simple an act as telling people what I loved and wanted to do could reap such a response.

Everything changed. I worked with the newly adventerous faculty helping them find ways to use murals, pup-

11

pets, or papier mache to enliven their curriculum. Suddenly, everyone was conscious that they could use these arts. There seemed to be an explosion of energy, like a critical mass, where the arts seemed to flower. There were murals about dinosaurs, plants, the study of evolution, the history of Chicago. A special education class made papier mache puppets and a puppet theater and then created plays. A second grade classroom made papier mache masks as the first step for a study of drama. A fourth grade teacher wanted help to celebrate the coming Chinese New Year. We made a papier mache dragon head, batiked banners and took to the streets with the banners and dragon in a joyous New Years celebration. I also gave workshops at 7:30 a.m. We talked about using these skills and how to incorporate them into their curriculum. Everyone plunged in and came up with an immense amount of creativity and vitality.

Groups of parents became aware that they could alter the physical environment. The excitement that was generated within the school overflowed, and the parents were recruited to become actively involved in designing the school walls. Years ago, the school walls had been painted institutional pea green, a color that left everyone feeling as drab and dull as the walls. We got together with the parents and talked about new colors and designs and then painted beautiful graphics on the walls. Not only did the parents become empowered by actually changing the physical environment, everyone in the school environment felt its effects.

I learned from this experience that revealing what I was interested in—not what I had knowledge of or was skilled at—was vital to learning. The fact that I did not know how to make murals, papier mache, or puppets was secondary. I could learn and did. My interest, my energy was the force that took us down a series of paths. I could deal with the surprises and could learn new skills because there was so much vitality generated. We all were able to open up to many new possibilities and together involve ourselves in a creative approach to learning.

It takes only one person to acknowledge what they love and everybody around them will want to learn. One person's enthusiasm is like a brush fire: It cannot help but spread. It usually starts with that first burst of knowing, that "ah-ha," when we are on to something. That "something" is our own energy, and that energy is our authentic self.

To begin working with our energy, we must honor its presence. It exists everywhere, but can only be known by experiencing it. This energy is honored throughout the world—as Ki in Japan, Chi in China, Kundalini in India, the Holy Spirit by Christians, the Void by Buddhists, Ruah by Jews. Even in secular America, we have created "the force." And we can't miss it in our lives. It surfaces mysteriously when we embrace an old friend and all thought lets go to reveal our uninhibited delight (ahhhhh-hhhhh), or when we watch a child laugh or cry with abandon; or when we fall into an unselfconscious space of love.

When we stop to sit and collect ourselves, we have a chance to connect with a more authentic part of ourselves.

We learn to listen and to experience our energy and our artistic expression—that small but insistent inner voice that heightens awareness and lightens our load.

When we have the courage to begin with that part of ourselves which knows—and knows that it knows—we are free to explore, to learn, to take risks, to make mistakes— all elements of creativity. Then it is really not the "what" of what we are doing that helps children learn; it is the spirit and boldness that we bring to it that creates the emotional bonding that makes learning stick. Our energy becomes the glue.

"Who Do You Love?"

A woman came to see the great nineteenth-century Indian mystic and realist, Ramakrishna, and told him that she did not love God.

"Who do you love?" he asked.

"My nephew," she replied.

"There God is," responded Ramakrishna.

What Ramakrishna pointed out to this woman was that her love of her nephew was indeed her love of God. And we might infer that whatever we love, whatever is interesting to us—what, in fact, "turns us on"—is what has real meaning for us.

Do we hesitate to believe the truth of this tale? Is it more comfortable to give our allegiance to the accepted patterns that have been imposed on us from our parents, neighborhood, workplace, churches or synagogues, or administrators than it is to resolve to accept ourselves as we are? Are we seekers after what we think other people value rather than after our own honest and alive center? Can we have the courage to accept that our highest nature is embedded in what and whom we love?

14

As this remarkable insight helped the woman in the story shift her understanding of where God might be, it could possibly help us open ourselves to what we love. And when we live from our passions, not only does a very different "us" emerge but also a very different—and effective—way of teaching.

PRACTICES

Henry David Thoreau was a great dreamer. He also suggested that in order for dreams to become realities, they needed a foundation:

> *If you have built castles in the air, your*
> *work need not be lost; that is where they*
> *should be. Now put foundations under*
> *them.*

We all have dreams of what we want to do or to become—or of how we might want to teach differently. Yet, without practice, these may remain only dreams. Without practice, we can't even be good swimmers, tennis players, or artists—much less good teachers. Our vision of a better way is grounded in practicing what we want to become. Although our dreams are our inspiration and keep us focused on our goals, we cannot just dream ourselves into being different. We need to see our habits of a lifetime, those conditioned attitudes that we *wish* we could change, to see how we sabotage our dreams. When we discover that old habits restrict us and our vision of who we want to become, we can begin to practice new, more desirable ones.

The difficulty with practice is that none of us wants to do it. We balk at practice because it is repetitious and boring. Our instincts are to want good things to happen to us without much effort. But we also know from experience

15

that when we do exert effort, a certain ease begins to flow into what we do and, ironically, what seemed difficult becomes effortless. When I swim, for example, the more I focus and continue practicing, the more facility I have. I am lifted out of the struggle and the striving to a place outside myself where I feel as if I am watching myself take one stroke after another. At these moments of freedom, I feel as if my body is being guided through the water. And there is a certainty and simplicity in my actions. I have become a vehicle for another force to take over and guide me from the inside out.

Practice produces this unique satisfaction. But this joy cannot accompany our actions without our effort at regular and consistent discipline. After we practice anything repeatedly for a long time, a remarkable thing begins to occur. We find that our attitudes have shifted into the ones we always yearned for, and we begin to experience our life as a gift rather than a continual set of problems to be solved. As we continue our practices, we also note that habits we had tried hard to either suppress or strip away have mysteriously disappeared. We find that we are becoming more of the person we wanted to become. And, if we are teachers, we find a new freshness. We are more aware of who we are in that role, and we approach teaching with an expanded understanding of what learning and creativity is all about. We become the beneficiaries of our increased awareness. And so do all the people we come in contact with—our fellow teachers, administrators, and, especially, the children.

The practices at the end of each chapter are provided to help you to continue the process of unfolding into your most honest and effective self. Many of them require time for reflection. Select the practices that fit you. In order to participate fully in these practices, you will need a journal or notebook in which to keep your reflections. They will aid you in doing these practices, and they will also be there as a reference for you to use as you proceed on this path of teaching from the inside out.

"You Don't Have to Drink Your Tomato Juice"

1) In a notebook or journal, write a list of twelve activities you love to do. Let them come up quickly without judging them. It could be as simple as having your first cup of coffee in the morning or watching a child play. Stay close to your own life, not what you think you're supposed to like. Then, prioritize them. What do you like best, next best, next . . . all the way to the least.

2) Describe in your journal a time when you followed someone else's values. Did it diminish or support you? How did you feel?

3) One way to notice your own gifts is to name a time when you were very excited about what you were doing. Close your eyes and go back in your memory to such a time. Where were you? Who was there? What was said? What did you do? How did you feel? Recreate the event by writing it down in your journal.

The Blocks: Stumbling or Building

1) Sit down and watch your breath as it goes in and out. Try to stay with the natural rhythm of your breath. When your mind wanders off, simply come back to your breath. Begin to notice your thoughts as they pass through your mind like clouds forming and dissolving in

17

the sky. Write your experience in your journal, but don't judge it. This could become a daily practice.

2) Discover what frightens you by writing in your journal the key phrases you use that limit you, such as "It's not fair" or "I can't do it." Make a list of them. How do you feel? Experience the frustration, anger, or tightness in your body. By experiencing your bodily sensations, your feelings will shift. Now write down their opposites, such as, "Everything happens for the best" or "I am capable." What have you discovered as you have done this practice? Write your discoveries in your journal.

3) Discover what fears arise when you do something creative by noticing and making notes about them in your journal.

Education: The Way It Is

1) Write in your journal some of the things you teach that you think are irrelevant. What might be more relevant to you? To your students? Note these ideas in your journal.

2) List your school's expectations for you and what you are supposed to teach. Then list your expectations for your self. Finally, list your expectations for your students.

3) What do you do during a typical day at school that bores you and/or bores the children? Sit quietly by yourself with this boring subject and feel your distaste and frustration. Now discard it and wait quietly to see what fills that void. Write about your experience of boredom and what you would like to replace it with.

18

Education: The Way It Could Be

1) Think of an activity you love that you are involved in outside of teaching. Feel the enthusiasm you have for this activity. How might you bring your interest in that activity into your teaching? Write in your journal five ideas that come to you. Don't worry about whether they are "possible."

2) Select one subject that you teach and imagine another way to teach it. Describe this in your journal.

3) Contemplate an ideal teaching environment. Let yourself dream about what that might look like, where it might be, what you would be doing and teaching. Give yourself permission to have whatever you want. After experiencing this in your mind's eye, write it down in your journal in detail. Go back later and read what you have written; add to it if you want to.

4) Carve out a time for yourself so you can stop and notice what is around you. Could you make something from whatever is there? Note in your journal the ideas that come to you.

Working With What Is Available

Going from Here to There

A friend of mine once questioned a monk. She asked how she would know if she were on the right path. He looked from right to left and from left to right as if he were trying to find it. Then he looked down at his feet.

"Why," he said, "just look at where your feet are. That's where the path is, right under your feet!"

There is no place else to begin except where you are, now, in the present moment, with the materials and ideas that are at hand. If we know where we are, we can take the next step—the one in the direction our heart leads us. If, on the other hand, we plan ahead or depend on what others tell us to do, we stray from our path and have to

21

ask that question again ... and again ...and again: How do I know if I'm on the right path?

Look down at your feet. Everything you need is right there.

Things Are Not What They Seem

An art teacher friend of mine saw hairnets in the five-and-dime one day. She bought one and started playing with it. She began to see all the ways the squares moved into diamonds and squinty-eyed slits as she stretched it this way and that, watching the lines make new shapes. "How can I use this in my art class?" she wondered. The next day, she tacked it to a white board in front of her art class and began to stretch it and tack it again. The children became fascinated; they began to see the hairnet not as a hairnet but as connecting lines that created wonderful shapes as it was stretched. The visual stimulation inspired the children to create abstract paintings, using lines like the hairnet across a large sheet of paper. Then they painted the spaces they had created. The paintings were beautiful. The inspiration: a hairnet, discovered by the teacher, by being here, now.

When we are attentive to the present moment, anything can happen. Things are not what they seem to be. When you can see paintings in hairnets, you can see possibilities anywhere! Look at a tree branch that splits into two arms reaching up. Pretend it just fell to the ground. Pick it up. Look at it. It's still a tree branch. Now turn it upside-down. What does it look like to you? Could that tree branch become legs, in your imagination, that might become a puppet by adding scraps of material or paint? The whole world is full of possibilities. Anything can be used to begin to see legs, eyes, abstractions, figures, houses. We need to turn off our logical, everyday mind that tells us, "Egg cartons are for eggs." What about egg cartons for caterpillars, eyes, baskets, ears, or cups?. When we find ourselves looking, really being aware of where we are, we can go a step at a time, discovering the possibilities as we go. We have to keep it simple and be attentive, as we walk from here to there.

Start by looking down at your feet. Where are you? Where is your school? What is the neighborhood like? What is outside your window? Be honest, be simple. Make a list. Start somewhere. Start where your feet are.

Seizing the Moment

Once I walked into a seventh grade classroom on the third floor of an old school on Chicago's southwest side. Through the windows I saw a sea of rooftops stretching as far as the eye could see.

"Wow, that is amazing," was my first response.

The teacher and I had previously discussed several possibilities of doing an art-related project in her classroom. However, after I saw the view outside the classroom window, my whole perspective shifted.

"What if we did something around these rooftops?" I asked the teacher.

"Why not," she agreed.

23

By seizing that moment, without knowing how it would proceed, we gave birth to a wonderful project. The rooftops became the source for examining a familiar scene, one that had been only background up to this moment. The students were inspired to explore rooftops right outside their own windows through poetry, through drawing, and through combining the two in "picture poems." The more everyone allowed themselves to explore, the more there was to see, to imagine and to know about these rooftops, and by extension, about all rooftops and about shelter, as well.

And when the writing and drawing were completed, I felt that the project was, as yet, incomplete and could be explored further. Another moment came when I thought that rooftop sculptures could

somehow be created, and we moved the project into another dimension. The rooftops continued to capture everyone's deepest creative expression. I was surprised that the children's interests—along with the teacher's and my own—accelerated to a new level of enthusiasm. Working with cardboard from packing boxes and masking tape, the children began constructing wonderful Chicago-style houses with stairs, porches and, of course, rooftops. When they finished constructing thier houses with papier-mâché and then painting them, they incorporated their "rooftop" poems into their sculptures by writing the poems on the sculpted rooftops.

This classroom came alive as the children immersed themselves in the scene right outside the window. I took the leap, the teacher responded, and the kids, bless them, rose joyfully and knowledgeably to the challenge.

The tools for creating art emerge from examining "the here." When we notice hairnets in the dime store, when

25

we examine ordinary rooftops outside our windows, we are already "here." When we become attentive to all the "heres" of our lives, each moment is full of promise.

Teaching Is Like Making a Salad

Like my friend, I also love to make salads. Looking into the refrigerator, I see what is there: half a green pepper, three pruney-looking radishes, some left-over noodles, sprouts, fresh kale with red veins, steamed cauliflower from last night's dinner. I haul them all out onto the kitchen counter. The color and shapes are exciting. I chop, tear—a little of this, some of that—as I fill my favorite cerulean bowl my mother-in-law made for me. I begin to see the color and shapes as the vegetables take on new forms: shades of red, green, white; shapes of ovals, rounds, squares, diagonals and up-and-down patterns from the curly leaves. I am delighted at my composition, and I feel grateful . . . and I am also hungry. I eat it and enjoy the mingling flavors. Then it is gone, but the creation and the eating of it were stimulating. The art of the salad was in the discovery—what happened to be available—and in the joy of putting it together. How simple. How ordinary. How unaware we usually are of what we are doing.

Teaching can be like making a salad. We can walk into the classroom and discover what is right in front of our noses. Who are these children? What kinds of houses do they live in? What is their ethnic background? Is there a child who is dying to tell you something important that you haven't had time to listen to? What are the particular ingredients that are there for you to work with? What kinds of windows do you have in your room? What do you see through them?

26

Let the houses across the street become more than just background scenery. Ask yourself (while you are asking the class) to imagine a life that goes on inside them. Have you seen people coming and going? Can you imagine their lives, how many children, aunts, uncles, grandparents, dogs, cats, goldfish, live there? What kinds of smells come from the kitchen? Give the family a name. Get specific. What do they wear? What are their voices like? The furniture? The paint? The wallpaper? What kind of toothpaste do they use? Building on everyone's imagination, write a class story on large cardboard pages and then illustrate it, adding a drawing from everyone. Create a sculpture of the house, like a dollhouse, inside and out. Call the project language arts, math, art, reading, writing — what you will. Call it curriculum if you want, but don't get stuck in it. The word is limiting. By trying out different words to describe what "curriculum" is, we can expand our definition of it. We can give it life, make it ours.

Perhaps the children in your classroom are of Spanish, Polish, Appalachian, African-American, Jewish, Protestant, Catholic, Hindu, or Muslim origin. Invite them to tell first-hand stories about their traditions, celebrations, families, foods, habits, lovings, hatings. Choose one of the holidays and celebrate it. What is needed? Make finding out about the celebration the goal. Have the children write reports, researching in the library, asking questions of people in the neighborhood. There is so much to know. Some of it the children will know in their memories, their bones, who they are, back for generations. Invite the memories to surface and encourage children to write about them—or paint them, if that feels safer. Do both. Collaborate in making the items needed to create

27

the celebration: candle sticks, flags, sculptures, bread. Now, tell the principal that you are doing a multi-cultural curriculum. Invite parents, relatives, other students to participate in the celebration.

You are supposed to study native Americans. How can you get yourself truly excited about Native Americans so that the students will feel your interest and therefore love studying Native Americans too? How do you crack that open for yourself? Start in a different place, not the textbook. Look up American Indians in the yellow pages and find out what's there. Write to the Bureau of Indian Affairs in Washington. Wherever you are living now, Indians once lived. Who are/were they? Their art, their customs. Write to native Americans if there aren't any in your community, and, if there are, visit them. Get their stories on a tape recorder. Hear what they say and how they say it so that you will understand in your heart as well as your head. Create a multi-faceted Indian project using stories, myths, ceremonies, music. Paint Indian tipi murals. Keep the energy alive and you will no doubt find something that you can connect with. From there, follow that thread.

Did the shy child who's been dying to tell you something for months finally tell you about his new baby sister who is already three months old but you didn't have time to listen? Don't pass over this moment. Use it. Announce this great news to the class and make something for the new baby for her big brother to take home to her: a mobile with animals or shapes, brightly colored so that the baby can watch and kick and coo and the children can learn about balance.

When I am an artist-in-residence in a school, I look for "ingredients" for uplifting curriculum in lots of places.

28

Sometimes I am the one who initiates an idea that fascinates me, and then it takes off, manifesting in many projects. Other times, the energy comes when I am listening to a child I am working with and I discover something that she is particularly interested in exploring. Together, we find ways of expressing it. Still other times, the energy comes from brainstorming with the children everything that we are interested in until a class consciousness surfaces and we have discovered what we want to do. Collectively, we are part of a greater whole that we have produced together. Sometimes the energy is not even in the topic itself but in the creative possibilities that we can all think of to make that topic come alive.

Wherever the source of the energy—from the artist, the teacher, or an entire classroom of children—when we allow it to sweep us off our feet, our voices, whether they be in paint, writing, drama, dance, music, or the basic curriculum, will "speak" with clarity and conviction.

The important key is to follow whatever energy is available to you in whatever ways you can because it is energy that produces joy, and joy that produces self-esteem, and self-esteem that allows us to learn. People do not learn much when they do not feel good about themselves. And when children are despondent for lack of energy, they are not interested in learning what others want them to learn.

There are so many wonderful kinds of salads waiting to be created, so many different kinds of curriculum to be made with just what is there, here, now.

Redefining Creativity

I once worked with a teacher named Jan and her fourth graders on several projects. We were talking about how we could take some striking portraits the children had made and make them visible for a special assembly audience in a large hall. Jan came up with the solution. She decided to requisition a video camera from the board of education, film the children's artwork, and play the video on a large screen for the assembly. Her ingenuity solved one problem, but it created another. Everyone would be able to see the portraits if she could learn how to use the video camera. She had never used one before. Naturally, she felt apprehensive about doing so.

One day not long after, Jan stopped me just outside her classroom to share her anxiety over learning, what seemed to her, a huge obstacle. She admitted that she didn't know what she was doing. "You seem to know what you're doing all the time," she commented, searching for a solution.

In a flash, the truth emerged. "I never do," I heard myself say.

I was as surprised by my statement as she was. I could tell her the truth: my story of anxious moments loaded with possibility, demonstrating that within ourselves we possess the confidence to solve each situation that arises. I explained that by being with a creative moment, I often don't know where to go, but that I trust I will be able to find out once I get there. There is a sense of adventure in the process and, while I am often anxious, trusting the process feels like an essential way of being.

It felt important to tell Jan my experience—that I didn't know what to do—and that not-knowing was a main ingredient of the creative process.

This story isn't a typical one about creativity, describing happily making something that would please us and others. Instead, it tells us that we are always presented with a "problem" where we must decide what to do, whether or not to seize that moment despite our not-knowing. And it also tells us that creativity isn't some lofty feeling or idea that only a few of us possess. When we idealize creativity, we separate artists from everyone else. Not only does that isolate artists and make them into something other than ordinary, but it also keeps the rest of us comfortably in our heads, not exploring, not playing with the material of our lives.

Eric Gill, an English craftsman, summed up our dilemma about who an artist is by telling us emphatically that "an artist is not a special kind of human being; every human being is a special kind of artist."

If we can allow that stunning statement to inspire us, we will find not only that creating is an ordinary activity, but that it also emerges from our everyday experience and is a part of our natural functioning. The "ordinariness" is what is special.

If creativity springs from the ordinary, we must allow the prescriptive to fade in order to broaden our perspectives. Discoveries come from the unexpected, when we are not attached to our own ideas.

There is a school for young children in Italy, called Reggio Emilia, that has evolved a philosophy of education based on observing children and how they can be guided into developing their massive potential—even at ages three to six. The teaching staff includes an *atelierista*, an artist. Together they create projects that are initiated by the children, yet meticulously guided by the adults. The consequence of much caring observation is a fully creative environment in which children are encouraged to greater levels of observation, followed by expression of their learning in a multitude of forms. Loris Malaguzzi, the

31

founder of Reggio Emilia, says that "creativity requires that the school of knowing find connections with the school of expressing, opening the doors to the hundred languages of children." Unlike the people in this unique environment, we may not be in one where we are supported to express our own creativity. However, we must sharpen our awareness and do what we can to help children with the exciting process of learning and expression.

When we think that creativity only belongs to artists, those we think "know" what they are doing, we come up short of our own natural talents. The studio is too limiting a place for all we have in us. Are we not artists in the classroom, in the kitchen, the lab, the garden, in life?

Unfortunately, this is a notion not commonly understood. We are a nation of specialists, and we define our roles with more and more specificity. Our limited definitions lack the common thread that binds all people together: the fact that we were born creative and still are, if we could accept that reality and live from it.

What usually passes for teaching is anything but creative. The school day doesn't look like a canvas with colors and forms or like a piece of music with themes and rhythms. It looks more like a ladder with rungs at regular intervals, a lock-step linear method proceeding upward toward a specific goal. If we would re-fashion that goal, perhaps by re-asking the important questions, the ladder would go and in its place would be a more creative and humanizing structure.

Teaching is a creative process like any of the accepted art forms—visual arts, music, dance, drama. The medium is different but the process is the same. Instead of painting by number or teaching by rote, we all have the opportunity at any moment to become aware of any situation

32

(which is the art material) and use it. Each moment is critical because we can choose between painting within the lines that someone else has made for us, or teaching what someone has told us to teach . . . or finding our own unique and expressive way through the material, making our own marks. The choice is always ours.

Every time we take a risk to be creative and express ourselves, we model that for the children. When they see us less guarded and more naturally ourselves—being in the moment, trying out new ideas—they see a way of being that is unhappily not modeled enough. Let's examine how strongly modeling affects us all.

Changing the Model

I grew up in a neighborhood where everyone mowed their lawns. That is the way I learned to take care of grass. That is what was modeled. That is what I accepted. That is what I did without ever giving it another thought, a thought such as, "Do I like grass anyway? If I do, would I like it long or short? Or would l like to grow flowers or a prairie in place of grass?" Nowhere was there even a sense that there might be a choice. I learned what the neighborhood taught me without anyone ever saying a thing. The model of green seamless lawns taught me not to question any further. A very powerful model.

"Model" is both a noun and a verb. The noun can mean an example for imitation or emulation; the verb, to shape or fashion in imitation of a particular model. Either way, passively or actively, modeling is the way we learn. We falsely imagine that we learn only if we are in a class. Everything teaches us: our homes, neighborhoods, towns, countries. Modeling may be both the most powerful concept in teaching and the one that is most often overlooked.

Too often schools model themselves after factories: well-oiled and purposeful. They turn out a commodity. It is hard to face that fact, but we, as a nation, want "standardized" kids. We think we want individuality, creativity, initiative, but we model a passive, "yes ma'am" quality. We insist on right answers. We don't want to rock the boat so we don't ask kids too much about what they feel, what they like, what they want. If we did, we would have very different kinds of schools and kids. The schools might be places that fostered more curiosity, more expression, more creativity, more kindness.

We may think we teach our children, our students, what they need to know. Actually, who we are teaches them. We cannot escape the enormous impact of who we are as the chief educator. Children are like sponges; they take in our kindness, our indifference, our uptightness. Whatever inner qualities we have are expressed in our behavior, in the ways we relate to others. That is what children learn. If we understood the power of our effect on others, we might spend more time cleaning up our own acts, teaching ourselves, instead of trying to put others straight.

If we look back at all the people in our lives who were important to us, we can pick out those who, in some way or other, modeled qualities we admired and approaches that felt good to us. Usually, they were people who were genuinely interested in us and who had something of their own to share. When we were with the people who touched us deeply, we could become more of who we were.

I remember Mrs. McNut, my fifth grade teacher, who led us all outside one day to look for monarch caterpillars to put into jars so we could watch them go through their magnificent metamorphosis. I loved going to school in the fifth grade, I loved Mrs. McNut, but I loved mostly that she invited me to become interested in real-life things. She gave my natural curiosity something to feed upon. I couldn't wait to get to school every day. I would stand at the windowsill watching each minute step of the caterpillar becoming a butterfly. That has stayed with me all these years and has given me a deep appreciation of life: how it changes and how I change, how life never stays the same, how important process is, how truly amazing life is, and how I can emulate that flow in my own life. Perhaps Mrs. McNut did not think she was teaching all that when she took us out to look for caterpillars. But she modeled what was truly important and interesting to her, and she gave me one of the great teachings of my life.

Asking Questions

As an artist who has worked with hundreds of teachers in their schools and classrooms, I have seen all kinds of teaching styles. The gap between what is most prevalent and what is possible is often painful.

The word "educate" is derived from the Latin, "educare": to lead out or to bring up. It implies drawing out one's hidden, latent, natural potential, discovering the innermost, unmasked person secretly hoping to unfold him or herself.

If this is the goal of education, we are a long way from realizing it in our schools, those institutions we allow our children to spend huge amounts of time in—while being molded to fit into—an agenda that is the antithesis of uncovering their natural potential. In my experience, school and teacher agendas, more often than not, try to "fill up" children with unrelated facts, like gas into a gas tank, rather than drawing out what is there inside the

35

child. There is more frustration than meaning for children and teachers in this approach, and we are a long way from making their day enjoyable or even interesting.

This chasm that exists between the goal of education and the reality of the schools could be bridged, step by baby step. We could begin to draw together our heads and our hearts and heal the violence that we inflict upon ourselves in the name of education. We need to ask ourselves the essential questions: To what goal? For what reason? We must begin at the beginning.

In one of the schools that I worked, I wanted to question the teachers to find out what they really loved and how curriculum might be made from their interests. When I asked Barb, a second grade teacher, what she liked to do best, she snarled at me as if I had intruded on her sacred teaching schedule.

"Don"t ask me that," she snapped, "I have to teach reading and math and . . . "

I interrupted. "I understand, but, let's just fantasize and pretend you could teach anything you wanted. What would that be?"

Barb relaxed and began to tell me about her love for drama and how she always went to the theater. She was even taking acting classes. She began opening up to me, to herself, and to her own curiosities. Together we began to develop ideas and activities around her fascination with theater. We made masks, wrote plays, created games to explore the five senses. It was wonderful, and Barb was thrilled with using material that interested her. She and the children became vibrant as they easily learned through doing activities that were both intellectual and expressive, and that contained multiple possibilities.

Teaching is a process that always starts with ques-

36

tions. Questions about what we are about as teachers, what this profession is about, and what it requires if we wish to be involved in it. Too many people in the educational profession do their jobs the way they are told, the way it has been done in the past. Unless we take time to focus on the children's real rather than perceived needs— and on our own—we will keep hitting the same wall in education that we have been hitting for a long time.

Perhaps administrators and teachers alike could formulate questions that might offer an entirely new framework to what it means to educate. Questions such as:

1) What are we doing in the schools, really? What do we want for our children, for our nation's children?

2) What kind of environment do we want for children? One that nurtures and supports the natural evolution of children, intellectually, creatively, and spiritually? Or one that deadens their curiosity?

3) Do we want students to participate in choosing what they want to explore?

4) What would happen if we allowed ourselves to fantasize about how we would really like to be as teachers? Do with children? What kind of day would we fashion? What kind of year? What would be its rhythms?

5) What is a classroom anyway? Where does it end? At the four walls? In the neighborhood? The city?

6) What's important to know? What's important to be?

7) Do we, in fact, want to think about these questions for ourselves or allow others to answer these questions for us? How do we give away our power and allow others to answer for us?

These are essential questions about the development of young lives and about our own growth. They need to be asked. They need to be pondered. Asking these kinds of questions might bring some surprising answers. Answers that bypass the "how-to-do-it" formulas, the curricula someone else created, the principal's expectations, even the janitors desire to keep the school clean at all costs (creativity, mostly). If we would contemplate our own fundamental questions about what we are doing, what someone else expects of us, and what we might do if we could, not censoring ourselves, we might find out all kinds of things about the nature of learning and what we could do to facilitate it.

Getting Support

When a potter throws a pot on a wheel, she must support it with both hands as it spins, the right hand on the outside holding the shape while the left hand is controlling the thickness on the inside. This support is essential to maintaining the walls of the fragile moist clay as the pot spins.

I love the image of the right hand outstretched in support, gently holding the shape of the pot while the left one pushes against the inner surface to thin the clay wall. It is an image about the way we are all formed. If there is strong support on the outside, it allows us to lean while we are shaped, knowing we will not collapse. And when there is a subtle and gentle push from the inside, we are

38

aware that the walls of our resistance can be thinned.

We do not grow without support. Nobody does. It is not possible. Teaching requires offering support to students all the time. Children need as much support as possible and teachers need to give it freely and abundantly. Support is a tonic that nurtures self-esteem, allowing us to take the necessary risks—the next steps into unknown and uncharted territory. We know that young people need warm, caring, nurturing environments and people in order to grow. We know that without it, a child sinks into a protective shell and does not have the confidence to learn.

But who supports the teachers? Mostly teachers are stashed away in their classrooms, isolated from one another, giving all day. Lack of teacher support is a recipe for stress and exhaustion. Teachers need to know their worth as creative people in order to stimulate the children's potential to care for themselves. Teachers need support, someone with whom to check out ideas and possibilities, someone to give balance so they can honestly reflect on what they are doing. Without supportive intervention, we are all prone to fall into the common collective complaint of how hard life is. While that may free up some of the pent-up frustration that is born of too much isolation, it will not allow us the freedom and inspiration a support system can offer.

Support can come from the inside. Ideally, there should be a supportive learning environment within every school. The best support may be your colleagues, other teachers who may be isolated, just like you. When teachers come together to share what they are doing with each other, they create an opportunity to listen empathically. Listening is one of the greatest supports we can give each other. When we listen to another, our differences and competition dissolve. Listening soothes a question, cools a dilemma, and diminishes differences with others who have similar questions and dilemmas. Without support we become isolated, and isolation builds walls between us and within us. We doubt our own marvelous capacities and are afraid of sharing our problems and solutions. Institutions that encourage and facilitate a system of support between colleagues strengthen the entire organism in the process.

Support can also come from the outside, such as when an artist comes in to work with a teacher. On a purely practical level, just another body in the classroom is support. But the greater support comes from knowing that another person cares about what happens in that classroom and will support that teacher's creative expansion. When we know we have an advocate cheering us on, we have more confidence in ourselves. When we feel acknowledged by another, we can do things we never thought possible. And one of the best things about confidence is that it is contagious. It can overtake an entire system, teachers supporting teachers.

A very good idea would be that there would be at least one artist in every school across America. It could be a visual artist, a musician, a dancer, or a theatre person. Besides knowing the skills and aesthetic of their art form, the artist would also have to know about how to work with teachers in a supportive way, while they are trying out new and, perhaps, wild things they have never even dreamed they could do. (See Appendix for how to work with teachers.) The mere presence of an artist in a school, working with individuals or groups of teachers, would allow for continuity, for large themes to develop, for all school art exhibitions where everyone would be able to learn from each other.

Recently, I worked with a group of teachers in a summer program. The teachers felt supported during the three weeks of the program, and their confidence grew to such an extent that they became empowered to create support systems within their schools. Two teachers from that program were so excited by what they had experienced from the artists during the summer that they decided to begin a support system at the beginning of the school year. They invited all the teachers in their school plus those from a neighboring school to an all-day Saturday workshop that they lead based on the material they had received during the summer. That kind of initiative goes a long way in stimulating support for the entire system. It is like taking a remedy that affects the immune system. The remedy simply catalyzes what already exists within the system to support and heal itself.

* * * * * *

Learning to be creative is a process. It's an ongoing path with no ultimate destination. On it, we simply use what is given to us to gather data. Gathering data is what we perceive, simply what is there—in us, in the children, in the environment. That noticing is our path, those moment-by-moment observations that quicken our perceptions and open us to our basic and natural creativity.

Can we imagine ourselves in a beautiful and supportive environment that we and the children have created as an expression of who we are and what we are learning, making a continual effort to stay with what is flowing through us, the kids, the curriculum? It's a challenge, no doubt, but the only real one worth taking.

41

PRACTICES

Going from Here to There

1) What is "here" for you right now? Examine where you are and what the possibilities are in your exact situation. Write in your journal five possibilities.

Things Are Not What They Seem

1) Take a careful look at all the things in front of you: coffee cup, pencil, lined paper, *The Herald Gazette*—whatever is there. Take one of these objects and think of some things to do with it other than its original function. For example, a pencil. Normally, it is a writing tool. But could it become a flag pole, a drumstick, or a texture by gluing many pencils of different colors and sizes to a surface creating a collage of shapes. Write in your journal the ideas that come to you.

Seizing the Moment

1) Take a good look at the environment inside and outside your classroom window. In your journal, make a list of what you see, noting details. What does the list say to you about the neighborhood or town in which you teach? Create a project using this list. It could be having the kids write about what they see, or finding out about how the street got its name, or discovering who lives in the neighborhood, or when the houses were built across the street. Let yourself and your students become more attuned to all the facets in your environment.

Teaching Is Like Making A Salad

1) Choose one child from your class. What do you think her/his interests are? Create three activities that

would use this child's interests. Keep a journal about how the child's learning develops and what you learn as you pursue the activities.

2) Listen carefully to the words that your students use. What words have the most meaning for them? Let the children tell you the words they love. Write the words down and ask your students to write and/or draw a story using those words. How is the energy different in those stories from the stories they write about topics of your choosing?

3) Help children notice their own interests by asking them to write down five things they love to do. Then have them choose the one they love the most. Make a class list of everyone's "number one" interest and see if there are common themes. You and the children could create an activity using these interests, such as making a mural.

For example, if a child says, "I love to play hockey," you might research hockey by looking at pictures, bringing in some hockey equipment, perhaps going to a hockey game. Have the children draw their observations as they take in information. Using the drawings, arrange them on a large paper and paint a mural about hockey.

Redefining Creativity

1) Take an oft-used recipe and make it without referring to the actual recipe. Add one or two new ingredients to perk it up, such as an herb or an unusual vegetable. You are being creative with your cooking.

2) Look at one item on your schedule for today. Let that activity into your consciousness and think about it

for a minute or two. How could you change a part of it by deleting or adding something?

3) Pick something that you don't know how to do but would like to learn about. It could be something mechanical that you've never done before and that totally mystifies you. Even if you think it's impossible to learn, write in your journal ten ways you could find out. Keep brainstorming until you have a rich selection of possibilities. Try one of them. If it opens up new possibilities, try one of those. If it doesn't, go on to another on your list.

Changing the Model

1) Who are your models? Think of one of them and write in your journal how that person has inspired you.

2) Name a person in your profession who is a model for you. What is it about this person that you admire and what is it that she or he has taught you by being who they are?

3) What qualities do you think that you model for your students?

Asking Questions

1) In your journal, write a dialogue with yourself describing "This is what I should be teaching" versus "This is how I'd like to teach."

2) What are your personal goals for educating a child? Write them down in your journal. Come back to them weekly and refine them by adding or subtracting ideas.

44

This is an important question that needs ongoing contemplation.

3) If you could fashion a school anyway you wanted, what would it look like? Where would it be? What kind of schedule would it have? What would a typical day be like? Answering this question for yourself could make big shifts in your priorities. Take your time answering it but don't neglect it because it seems so big. Give yourself mental space to address this question.

4) What do you think knowledge is? Record your thoughts in your journal.

5) Think of the entire span of time from kindergarten through high school. A child grows up in those years. What do you think a child should know by the time he or she leaves high school? Let your mind wander over this question before you answer it.

Getting Support

1) What are your expectations of yourself? What is the reality of your situation? How can you be the best you can within that reality?

2) Do you feel supported in your workplace? If not, what are the conditions that keep people from supporting one another. If you do feel supported, explain how it works for you and your colleagues.

3) What (additional) structures could you suggest that would create a supportive learning environment where you work?

4) Envision your school as a supportive learning environment in which teachers share their best teaching strategies as well as their failures. Consider creating a forum in your school in which teachers could gather to share their talents, facilitating one another's professional development and creativity. Describe in your journal how that might happen.

5) Contemplate your relationships to the other teachers in your school. How supportive are your relationships? Do you assist them in their search for creative ways to teach? Do you hold back your creative ideas? Do you listen?

The Eight-Fold Path of Teaching from the Inside Out

The Eight-Fold Path

When Sylvia Ashton-Warner, the inspired teacher who worked with four- and five-year-old Maori children in New Zealand, first arrived in a Maori village to teach, she was armed with orthodox English "how-to-do-it" text books, with a vocabulary in English—not Maori. The texts were full of sentences involving indifferent words, such as, "Janet/John come look and see the boats . . . little dog run," accompanied by pictures of blond, blue-eyed children in front of houses with picket fences. The Maori children balked at these unfamiliar, bland, and unemotional words and sentences and would not learn to read them. Rather than meeting this situation with the present-day

47

tendency to label the children as "learning disabled" or "behavior disordered," Ashton-Warner took an imaginative and creative leap: She simply discarded the lesson plans, charts, and readers and began at the beginning.

She listened to the children. She became the learner, not the teacher. She came to understand that children's early words had intense meaning for them. Trusting that the children's own words would be sufficient for their initial reading vocabulary, she created a wonderful game. When the children were ready, they would, one at a time, whisper any word they wanted into their teacher's ear: "jet" because this child loved them, "house" from an overdisciplined girl, "bomb" from a violent boy. The teacher-become-learner simply wrote each secret word onto a sturdy cardboard square and gave it to the child. As the game developed, these little cards multiplied and became the children's personal books, and the children felt empowered by the fact that they had authored their own primers. As if by magic, they began to read.

This story illustrates how a sensitive and imaginative teacher can reach her students by listening to them—to their words and to their feelings about these words. Sensing the children's enthusiasm, Ashton-Warner created a simple and natural vehicle through which their learning could be awakened. She might have been a teacher with all the "right" text books, but she chose another way. She became the facilitator for the children's impassioned interests to emerge. She taught from the inside out.

What could we do to turn ourselves around, know our own passions, and be attentive to those of our students? In Ashton-Warner's book *Teacher*, it becomes evident that she possessed several qualities that helped her meet this

situation the way she did:
- she was sensitive;
- she had courage;
- she was comfortable with "not-knowing";
- she was willing to take risks;
- she was willing to listen;
- she paid attention;
- she trusted;
- she took time for reflection.

I want to examine these attitudes, one at a time, to see their relevance for teaching.

Sensitivity

Our culture is full of activity. We deify it. Being busy is what we aim to be. Ultimately, this desensitizes us. In schools, as I have encountered them, the schedule is so full and everyone is so pressured that time out for being with oneself or with a child is not a priority. If we could, instead, allow ourselves space to observe a situation as it presents itself, that would be sensitive. When Sylvia Ashton-Warner stopped to consider her situation, she understood that English primers were not going to help the children learn to read. She was sensitive to the fact that they could not learn from something they could not relate to. Like Ashton-Warner, if we could have the courage to stop when we do not know how to proceed and take in the situation, that moment would allow room for wisdom to emerge. Just stopping is being sensitive.

All life has rhythm. Our breath goes in and out. When we are sensitive to our breathing, we can notice a pause between each breath. Seasons change. There are times for growing, for reaping, for dying, for quiet. When we speed

49

up and do not honor our natural rhythms, we do violence to ourselves and others. Our sensitivity vanishes as we armor ourselves with old habits, assuming we are "right" and insisting our opinions and rules are the ones to be followed. We end up trading our sensitivity for aggression and forcing children to do what we want, violating their natural rhythms. And . . . we lose ourselves in the process.

We do not have to force ourselves on our curriculum, on our kids, on ourselves. We could begin to notice the times when we pause. When we become more sensitive to the natural pauses that allow us time to respond, we can make better choices about how to proceed—in the classroom, with a child, at any crossroad we come to. Pausing gives us time for things that are important to us.

Pausing each morning to look at ourselves in the mirror may be so obvious that it sounds silly to talk about it as a significant act. But it is! We look in the mirror and decide how we like what we just arranged on our bodies. We check to see if the earrings or tie or sweater we just put on looks good with our blouse or shirt. And our hair? How is it? Too long? Too short? We pause, we look, we consider the next move. It is important to us to see how we look each day. We have to notice where we are and start there. Once we understand that this look in the mirror is simple "pausing," we can begin "pausing" anywhere. And each time we do this, we enter the process of being sensitive to ourselves and those around us.

I am reminded of a teacher who was attempting to give a standard lesson on the "seasons" while a wild Midwestern thunderstorm raged outside. (The full account of this story is in the Introduction.) Instead of being sensitive to the storm, to the children, to herself, she was focused on filling up the remaining half hour left

50

before school ended. If she had been able to be sensitive to her environment, she would have been able to see the thunderstorm as an opportunity rather than an annoyance. If she could also have paused, allowing herself a moment to take in the power of the storm, she might have found in it an inspiration for teaching. And certainly, she would have noticed the children glued to the windows, unable to contain their curiosity and excitement. Pausing to notice the children, their interests, and perhaps even allowing herself the joy of the thunderstorm happening to everyone, she might have made a different choice. Pausing, she would have had a choice.

These days, the word "sensitive" has almost become devoid of meaning because it is so overused. We could reflect and redefine it, reexamine it, rediscover it so that we could begin to appreciate its special quality. All these "re's" emphasize the need to do again: to look again, to examine again, to discover anew, and to learn as though for the first time. There is no formula for cultivating sensitivity. It is a practice of noticing, and it expands through concentration. Each time we stop to begin again, we increase our awareness, which is what sensitivity breeds in us. Awareness allows us to deal with situations that arise from a natural, intuitive place rather than from a controlled and programmed agenda. Sensitivity allows a classroom to be a very delicate weaving, where interests of the students and those of the teacher are respected and woven together in a unique pattern.

Courage

We—the teachers and I—had this great idea. The kids could make banners out of headlines they wrote.

I was the artist-in-residence at Central Junior High

51

School. The faculty had chosen the theme of the twenties and thirties, and I was brainstorming with groups of teachers about themes the students could research. From this research, the students would create images of the times. Then we would bring all the artwork from the various themes together to create a massive art exhibit that would visually tell about these two decades.

One team choose the theme, "headlines of the times." The plan was for kids to write their own headlines and then paint them with black paint on two-feet wide banners that we would string around the school. As I was talking with this particular group of teachers, I sensed some hesitancy about letting the students paint their own headlines. One of the teachers suggested that the headlines be done on a computer. I had this sinking feeling, a feeling I always get when people get stuck with a formula of how the work should look before they even begin. I knew that using a computer to make the headlines would take the life out of this project. I suggested that computer lettering did not present a creative challenge for the kids. The results would not have the quirky and energetic look that children's hand lettering would. Besides, I offered, by hand-lettering the banners, the kids would have the experience of seeing letters as shapes. I even suggested the banners might look like giant poems.

One of the teachers patiently explained to me that the work should "look good" and that computers would do what the kids could not—make everything even. They were worried that the parents would see their kids work as "messy" and not like it. I began to understand that the teachers experienced the parents as putting pressure on them to present the children's artwork as clean and orderly. Sadly, these teachers lacked the courage to discover for themselves what they and the children expected the artwork to be. They had sold out. They simply wanted to please.

It is this "wanting to please" that robs us of courage, drives away our original ideas and our enthusiasm. Rollo May has said in his book *The Courage to Create*, "If you do not express your own original ideas, if you do not listen to your own being, you will have betrayed yourself. Also you will have betrayed our community in failing to make your contribution to the whole." (pp. 12-13)

The courage needed to speak our own truth takes heart. In fact, the word "courage" has in it the French word "coeur," meaning "heart." Courage is very definitely an inside job. Outside pressure needs to be discarded at least until we have examined what it is we think and feel. It takes no courage to please someone else. It takes great courage to honor our own feelings and ideas.

I always thought that the cowardly lion in *The Wizard of Oz* was a wimp. He was afraid of everything and every-one, but he did not like being afraid. So he traveled to see the great wizard who, he thought, would give him the courage lions were supposed to have. But the wizard, of course, turned out to be the lion's own wisest self—not a little man behind a curtain. When the cowardly lion con-nected with his inner self, instead of turning his attention outside where he was buffeted by others, he got what he wanted. Then he was able to use his authentic voice and roar like the majestic lion that he really was.

Having courage is a prerequisite for being creative. Like Sylvia Ashton-Warner, who had the courage to act in a situation in which she did not have the answers, we can-not march to someone else's drumbeat if we want to cre-ate our own lives. We need to explore in our deepest selves

53

to find out what we want to express. In our schools, where there is so much emphasis on conformity, it is especially essential to have courage to "do your own thing." As we have the courage to be our own selves, we will also be modeling courage to the children to be their own selves, to be all that they can be.

Not Knowing

"I don't know what to do. I don't know how to do that. I don't know what that means. I can't figure it out. I just don't know."

How difficult it is to admit our not-knowing. We all want to be right.

In school we are awarded for being right, and we learn to feel fabulous when we are. Our egos expand when we are right and others are wrong. We feel different and better-than. We know and . . . we know that we know.

Teachers through the ages have reinforced being right. "Who has the answer?" we teachers call out to a room full of children. The answer, the one right answer, the one right way to the truth. The children who know raise their hands to offer the right answer and to be praised for knowing it. The children who do not know— who learn differently, who do not hold on to facts so well—hope they will not be called on. We have taught what we did not expect to teach, did not even want to teach: We have taught young children that knowing makes us better than others and that if we do not have the answer, we are not very good or smart or nice—or something. We have taught children to feel and think poorly about themselves.

I do not think this outcome is what anyone ever meant to teach, but without reflecting on what and how

54

we are teaching, we have not allowed ourselves the opportunity to teach for a different purpose, to teach from the inside out. We—and our students—can learn from a different space, a space of wanting to know because we wish to know the secrets of life. We can thirst after a real knowledge that does not just inform us but also teaches us how to live our lives.

Imagine, for a moment, what it might be like to do as Sylvia Ashton-Warner did: to allow ourselves to stay in an insecure place until something else emerged. By taking the time, we might become wise enough to know that we have become narrow-minded. We might then have an opportunity to find another way to facilitate children's learning, a way that would allow each child to feel that she or he knew what they knew and that knowing was enough, and that each child was enough—even wonderful.

Philosophers from every culture talk about not-knowing as a path to wisdom. When we can cultivate an attitude of not-knowing the way the ancients taught it, we can see that learning is for ourselves, not for display. When we can learn for ourselves, we can go about our lives satisfied with what we know and with who we are instead of, as our system has taught us, learning to please others and then trying to impress them with what we know. Not-knowing can bring us to a deeper place of knowing. Inside.

I love to be prepared when I teach, to know what I'm doing, at least to have a plan. But, more and more, I have only an outline, and how an activity actually proceeds must evolve without my knowing how it will manifest. Recently, I was teaching a group of teachers about how to create projects that would enhance their students' awareness of specific artworks. The workshop involved collect-

55

ing data about what they saw in a specific painting, in this case, Georgia O'Keeffe's huge eight-by-twenty-four foot painting "Sky Over Clouds." I had prepared a general process: after writing about clouds the teachers had seen from airplanes and contemplating and drawing shapes of clouds, they were to cut out cloud shapes from large pieces of foamboard. There were four groups of clouds, from large to small. I asked them to hang the clouds from the ceiling pipes in the room. I thought the effect would be a wonderful way to further understand Georgia O'Keeffe's painting, but I didn't know how the clouds would hang to give a "Sky Over Clouds" effect. Someone asked me, while the clouds were scattered all over the room, if I knew how this would work.

"No," I told her, "you all have to figure it out."

The buzz in the room while the teachers cut, then organized, and finally hung the clouds told me that they were able to solve their own problems with interest and enthusiasm. When the clouds were suspended, we were in awe of them—and ourselves, for having discovered how to create an effect of clouds in the sky without knowing how it would work.

The heart of creative growth comes from our ability to let go of preconceived ideas and leap into the unknown. It is in the unknown where we first sense our resistances. Once we acknowledge our resistances by noticing the tightness in our body, a whole new landscape opens up—a fertile place in which we feel more deeply and sense ourselves from our bellies and hearts. It is our heads that imprison us, incessantly questioning, doubting, analyzing, organizing.

"Not knowing is the condition which makes us continue to search,"[1] said Loris Malaguzzi, founder of the unique art-related educational program in Reggio Emilla, Italy. As teachers, he goes on to say, the quality of not-knowing opens us up to the children and to the environment. Everything and everyone becomes a clue and an adventure to learning. The space of not-knowing creates a humility that helps us receive. We become soft and pliable. When we have left our "know-it-all" teacher stance, we are ready to learn. Then we can join the children as learners, and together we can teach each other.

[1] *The Hundred Languages of Children: The Reggio Emilia Approach to Early Childhood Education*, edited by Carolyn Edwards, Lella Gandin, and George Forman. Ablex Publishing Corporation, Norwood, New Jersey, 1993, pp. 86

Risk

Being with risk moment-by-moment is what life is about. Any time we move from our comfort zone into the unknown, we face potential threat and fear. How can we meet discomfort and not shrink from it?

One summer I was a teaching artist in a pilot program on the arts for teachers in Chicago. There were three other artists in the group—a dancer, an actor, and a musician—and together we worked with twenty-five public school teachers. Each artist was to present several workshops, and I was terrified when it was my turn. I thought that I might not have anything worth sharing, that everyone would laugh at me. I knew the other artists were wonderful. How was I ever chosen for this work, anyway? My mind would not stop. So, to compensate for what I did not think I knew, I worked hard to gather information for my presentation.

The day came. I arrived early at the studio and arranged everything. The teachers arrived. I was ready to begin. But when I went to get my notes out of my black briefcase on the table in the corner, I couldn't find them. I stopped. I was about to panic when this incredible sense of liberation filled me. I would just have to be myself. Whatever I knew, whoever I was at this moment, would have to do. I started talking and the ideas seemed almost to form themselves. I felt wonderful. As I began remembering the material I had worked so hard to gather, I started playing with it, talking about what I knew in my bones.

I discovered that I knew more than I thought. But even more important than that, I found that by simply doing the next thing, my fear was no longer blocking me. By taking the risk to begin, there it was, my knowledge and creativity, streaming out of me. I could do it. Just by being there, being present, and taking the first step, I gained the confidence I needed to move on.

When we know or imagine that someone or something will hurt us, we allow our fear to stop us. We freeze, unable to continue. But when we can allow ourselves to be with our stiffness in our bodies, really feel it, we can step forward anyway. Then, we are free. The steps of risk-taking are like the small steps of our daily lives: getting up in the morning, continuing to make our breakfast and our plans, continuing to sort out our priorities. We do not need to do everything at once, or imagine what the outcome will be. We simply need to get up and do it, one moment at a time.

What would happen if, like Sylvia Ashton-Warner, we could consciously cultivate an attitude of risk in our teaching?

She risked an unpredictable outcome when she resisted bringing pre-determined "right answers" into the classroom simply to quell her own anxiety. She risked NOT controlling the situation. What would happen if, instead of being bound by the curriculum that has been handed down from the "curriculum developers," we could step forward and teach our way. That would be a risk, to teach the way we really feel about whatever we are teaching. It would mean trusting that we know, that we have ourselves to share, and that within us is the richness that is the richness in everyone. And, if we risked sharing it, we could make a connection with the children that they would remember in the cells of their bodies their whole lives. When we allow ourselves to risk, we begin a discovery that takes us, and the children we are teaching, on a journey that is wonderfully unpredictable and that will continue to be the source for exploration.

I used to teach art at a small pioneer school for children with learning disabilities. I had been going along in a rather hum-drum manner week to week doing unrelated projects. One morning as I was waking, I began thinking about what I would do that day. Suddenly I thought of the clay that had been in the art room for ages. I pictured using it to make heads, possibly as a first step in making marionettes. I did not know the first thing about making marionettes, but that did not stop this idea from appearing during that quiet space between sleep and wakefulness. I jumped out of bed, excited and eager to get to school.

That day the children made clay heads, and when everyone had left at the end of the day, I sat staring at the heads. I knew then that I had committed myself to doing whatever was necessary to materialize marionettes. As

59

the weeks went on and we created more and more pieces for what I hoped would become marionettes, I pushed against my fear. The classroom drawers became full of body parts: clay heads, hands and feet, papier mache bodies, jointed legs and arms made from cardboard. I went from week to week, from body part to body part, hoping—risking— that somehow all these pieces would come together.

Had I known how to make marionettes, I might have become bored with the project. Instead, I was filled with the risk and thrilled with the outcome. The children, too, seemed excited as this process unfolded. When the day finally came that they were able to string the body parts together to complete their marionettes, they had a sense of "coming together" themselves, an unintended discovery and a great accomplishment for those children. I had a deep satisfaction that I had stretched myself and become more than I had ever thought possible. Scary? Yes. Worth the risk? Definitely.

Listening

Listening is one of the greatest gifts that we can give another person. We know when we have really been listened to, when someone takes us in. When they respect us enough to listen uncritically, we respect ourselves. When someone offers their complete attention, we know we are honored and valued.

How often does this occur in your life? I know that the times that I have felt listened to are far fewer than the times I speak to others. I know also that I do not always listen to others with the attention they deserve, the way I would like to be listened to.

Take a few minutes to do a simple exercise to experience a deeper potential in everyday listening. Take a notebook or writing pad and step out of your home, office, or classroom—out onto the streets. Listen. Listen to the wind, the cars, the people, the laughter, the screams, the clanking, the pinging—whatever you hear. Continue focusing on the sounds. Now, stand in one place and write down everything you hear. Then listen again. There is more to hear. Go into the sounds, listen to the quality of each sound. When you do that, you can take the sound in, you can bypass the minor annoyances that cross your thoughts, like remembering you need to clean out the refrigerator.

Do not let your mind intrude and begin chattering at you: "You know you should really get going. You have so much to do. This exercise is stupid. It's not getting me anywhere." This kind of chattering is what is called "monkey mind" in the Zen and Indian traditions: the mind that takes us away from the present. It is this chattering that keeps us constantly moving, or living in the past or the future, or telling us that we are not doing it right. And the worst thing about "monkey mind" is that it never shuts up. But we can become friends with it and know it for what it is: a mind with all kinds of impres-

sions and desires. With that knowledge and much practice, the chattering quiets down, and we are able to listen.

What was this listening experience like for you? If you
had a hard time doing this exercise, do not be discour-
aged. Listening is a skill and requires practice so our monkey minds do not take us away from what is happening in
the moment.

We tend to think that listening happens only with our
ears. Have you ever watched the way children listen?
They listen with their entire bodies. There is total absorption, a kind of immersion into the present—not even a
flicker of movement away from what is happening right
now.

I experience this kind of absorption when I am painting. There is something about engaging the hand and the
eye that keeps the mind quiet, allowing absorption to take
place. I see this in children, too, when they are absorbed
in creating. Distractions disappear while they listen and
become one with what they are doing. They are "gone,"
lost in their experience.

An artist friend of mine who works in the public
schools calls this "the look." She photographs children
while they are working. Having looked at many pictures
of children making art, she has noticed that they all have
a similar expression. They do not look self-conscious, the
way we often do when we know that our pictures are
being taken. Instead, they have a look of innocence, of
being with themselves, a look that we may remember
from times when concentration swept over us like a
breeze and we were at its mercy.

What is so important about full-body listening in our
teaching is that we need this kind of listening skill in
order to hear each child—not just what they are saying

verbally, but what they are saying with their bodies, with their expressions. And we need to listen to what they are saying AND what they are not saying. This is an important, but sometimes difficult, task. We can begin by listening to ourselves, by practicing keeping our chattering minds separate from our attention on what we are doing, by keeping our analyzing/evaluating minds separate from our focus. Then we can create some space for ourselves to recognize our genuine intuitions and responses. As we practice listening, this skill will spill over to hearing sounds, and, best of all, to hearing other human beings who hunger after being listened to. Then, like Sylvia Ashton-Warner, we will be able to really hear what the children are saying.

Attention

How often adults say to children, "Pay attention!" What we usually mean when we use that expression is that we want the children to stop thinking about anything else except what we are telling them at that moment.

In the army, it is "A - A - TENNNNN - SHUN." Snap to. No alternative. Look as though you are interested. What you think about is of no concern so long as you have that fixed look.

In the classroom, when a teacher cuts the chatter by calling, "Attention," it is an opportunity for students to empty their minds of separate thoughts and draw together on the same one.

The kind of attention that I am talking about is a little like listening, but also different. It is what Sylvia Ashton-Warner did after she threw away all the English readers and stood there naked and unarmed, without a new recipe for her "little ones." How would she know

63

what to do next without being attentive to herself first, to an inner quiet place from which she could see and begin to understand what the children needed? That inner focus comes through the heart where we feel connected to others. Had she simply "paid attention" in the way we usually pay attention, she might have invented another curriculum as equally uninspiring to this group of children as the original English primers.

I think of the many classrooms I have been in where real attention is not being paid, where children are simply performing preordained tasks that may or may not have anything to do with the kind of learning that would inspire them to further stretch themselves. I do not think that real attention can be focused toward others until we apply it to ourselves. When we can observe our own needs sufficiently, we can then create an opening from which we can hear and understand another. I believe that is what Ashton-Warner did: She paid attention to her inner-self first, and then she could be attentive to what was important to the children: their words and what those words meant to them.

Drawing is a skill of paying attention. It is about noticing, observing, investigating what is simply there. What do you see? Simply see it and record it. Don't express it or interpret it. In a drawing class I was teaching one time, I gave everyone an apple to draw. No problem. Everyone knows what an apple looks like and could easily draw one without looking. Then I asked everyone to take a bite from their apples and then draw it. Now there was a whole different configuration, and the eye had to pay minute attention to all the peaks and valleys of the "bite," without wandering. Then, another bite, and another drawing—and more, until the apple core was left and

64

attention had grown keener and keener with each drawing.

If you look up "inattentiveness" in a thesaurus, you will find such synonyms as "inconsideration," "disregard," "want of thought," "neglect." These speak mountains about their opposite, attentiveness, and what it might truly mean to be "considerate," have "regard" for another, be "thoughtful" and full of care ("careful"). Paying attention is a great skill, and it takes a lifetime of developing. But without it we become scattered and our energy dissipates. Without it, we are being inconsiderate, neglectful, disregarding, or thoughtless of others. Surely this is a wake-up call to pay more attention to paying attention.

Trust

During a workshop led by a dancer friend of mine, each participant was asked to fall into the arms of several people who would then lift the person up over their heads and carry him around the room. This was an exercise in trust and required all of us, when it was our turn, to give up our fear for that moment, to let go so that we could give ourselves to the others while they, in turn, supported our weight. When it was my turn to be lifted over the heads of my fellow workshop participants, I at first felt afraid. My habitual mode of not trusting the world surfaced without my knowing. With encouragement and support, however, I began to soften until I felt as light as a feather. I relaxed into a timeless moment. There was no holding on or back, no wondering if they would support my weight. I trusted that they would do their part in making this combined effort work. Each of us had a task to perform, but the only requirement for the carried person was simply to trust.

When the exercise was complete, what was revealing to all of us was that we felt as though we had become a unit in which all the parts functioned together. Our differences had melted and we moved as a team, in harmony.

What can we learn from this? Perhaps, we could believe that if we dropped our defenses, we could work more in harmony with a whole situation, become a piece of it. Instead of fighting the forces against us, creating tension and stress, we could trust, even in the most aggravating of circumstances, that what is happening is okay. Trust is probably the most difficult attitude to cultivate because it requires a foundation of belief that the universe—who we are in it and what is happening at any given moment—has its own perfection. Moments of confusion are the hardest to trust because at those times we are desperate to find a way out of our predicament of discomfort.

Consider Sylvia Ashton-Warner in a foreign environment, unable to establish learning with the books she had brought with her and then throwing those approved-of learning tools away and trusting that something would come. She was able to trust the risky process of waiting until something in her would know the right way to proceed.

Trust does not come easily, yet to live fully we need to develop a trust that we are part of a whole, part of nature. Like the lilies of the field that Jesus described as neither having to toil or spin for their clothing, we need to trust that we have an indispensable place in this vast universe. Like the snowflake that falls freely and accepts the wind to blow it where it will, we need to trust that where we land will be okay.

We all want to trust, but as infants, we learned that

the world was not an entirely safe place. We felt betrayed by our world in one way or another; Mom and Dad weren't always there, and we couldn't have what we wanted all the time. Consequently, we probably have more or less difficulty with trust as adults. We have become protective and have learned to hide our authentic selves from others, as well as ourselves. We have learned not to ask for help and not to share our thoughts and feelings. It is safer to do what others expect of us. In that way our craving for approval can be satisfied.

This is a predicament that we are all in. If we want to become trusting people, the journey must begin with ourselves. We cannot trust others until we begin listening to our own authentic voice.

Sometimes that voice is hidden when we are tired or preoccupied. A friend of mine who taught third grade told me that her students responded to her and to what she was teaching to the degree that she trusted them. When she was tired and did not have much patience with normal childlike behavior, her anxiety made them wary, and they reacted by not opening up to her. But when she was rested and relaxed, they could be themselves, and she could teach to their individual learning styles without being annoyed by their behavior. The children's behavior mirrored her trust level.

Trust doesn't come easily to us, but we can begin to trust our own uniqueness. There is no one just like us in this universe. Trusting mean to experience feelings that we don't like and want to avoid. If, over time, we can face those parts of ourselves that we don't show the world, and learn to honor and respect them, we enlarge our humanity and our capacity to honor and respect and trust others. As we become less protective and more trusting, that trust is reflected back to us. Maybe, by trusting that the children in our classrooms are doing the best they can with what they've been given and are not "bad," that trust will be returned to us. It's a balancing act learning to trust ourselves, others, and the universe.

Reflection

I was working on six-feet-tall wooden cut-outs of flowers. They were bigger than anything I had ever worked on. Each part of these cut-outs was painted in great detail. For instance, I painted the tiny blossoms of a prairie flower called Butterfly Weed, whose flower head is composed of a group of tiny orange blossoms. I got totally immersed in how each petal manifests and what its relationship is to the rest of the flowers. My vision narrowed while I caressed the details. After working like this for a while, I put my piece against a wall and stepped back to let my eye wander over the whole of it. I just stood there looking, absorbing the colors and shapes that played across the surface. I became very quiet.

This kind of "stepping back" is reflection, and it is an indispensable part of painting. Sometimes I have an immediate response. I can hear myself say, "That's beautiful." Then I know that I am on the right track and that how I have been painting—the colors, the forms, the way I have laid on the paint—is working. I go on renewed, knowing that the path I have been walking is a good one. Other times, I look and I feel an "ugh," a let-down. I know that the colors and forms are not working, and I continue looking, taking in the whole, until I have a sense of what to do next, which piece of the whole to begin painting again.

Artists know about reflection. We even have a fancy

name for it: critique. Most people are sure that a critique has everything to do with criticism. "These are all the things that are wrong with your painting." Or your writing. Or, heaven forbid, your character. Kids do not like criticism. Neither do adults. Who would? Especially if we think that everything we make or write or are is going to be ripped apart.

But, reflection is not about passing judgment. Reflection is looking at the whole and asking what is there. Reflection is as invaluable to teaching as it is to painting. It was Sylvia Ashton-Warner's ability to pull back and reflect on her entire situation that allowed her to see a bigger picture and possibility for her students.

Taking time to reflect can give young students a whole new perspective on what they have done. In Laurie's first grade class, we were making kites out of paper bags as part of an exploration of Japanese culture. The six-year-olds were creating images of anything and everything in the sky—leaves, clouds, the sun, insects, the moon, rain, snow, Superman, witches, ghosts—and painting them with tempera paints. As Laurie and I walked among the children, who were lying on the floor painting, we could see how powerful the paintings were. But the kids could not. They were focused on painting their own kites.

One day, before the kites were completely finished, I said to Laurie, "Let's have a critique. The kids need to stop, to look, to see what they have accomplished and what the others have done as well."

So we took all the kites and taped or tacked them to the board in the front of the room, making a group composition that was filled with color and the composite images of "what's in the air."

Everyone looked at the wall of kites, and there was a satisfied "ahhhhhhh" that filled the classroom. By stepping back, not only could each child see his or her own kite, but they could see all of the kites together. Everyone's perception of the kite project expanded.

After acknowledging everyone's appreciation, I began to explain what a critique, or reflection, was by reminding them what they already knew about critiques from an everyday experience, like looking in the mirror. I mimicked how we look at ourselves when we dress. The children watched me knowingly as I pointed out how we see what is there: our hair, clothes, earrings. If we do not like how the red-and-white-checked shirt matches our black corduroy pants, or how our hair looks, we change into our black-and-white striped shirt with the outstanding yellow collar and comb our hair back from our face. Then we take another look. We approve. We strike a pose. We like the changes we have made.

The children smiled understandingly, knowing what I was talking about, and I told them that looking in the mirror is like critiquing artwork. We could simply look at our work and see what was there. And see if we wanted to change anything.

Then I pointed to Steven's kite and asked everyone, "What do you see?"

"A ghost," answered Katy.

"What kind of ghost?"

"A white one. Wel-l-l-l, it's sort of grey and the eyes are really big."

"Does it fill the paper?"

"Yeah, but it's hard to see."

"What do you think could be done to make the ghost easier to see?" I asked.

70

"He could outline it," Joe responded.

"That's a great idea. What else could he do to make the ghost easier to see?"

Hands flew in the air. "Maybe the sky could be black 'cuz ghosts fly at night," said Renaldo, who seemed to be an expert on ghosts.

"That's good, Renaldo. Also, the black would really make the ghost stand out, wouldn't it?"

Steven was sitting there taking all this in. I turned to him and asked him what he thought.

"I think I'm going to paint the sky black and maybe outline the ghost with red."

Steven was satisfied. He had a plan. We moved on, critiquing someone else's kite. I continued asking the children what they saw, and they responded, clarifying their answers so that we all could understand and see more than we saw before.

In this situation, everyone learned about composition, color, balance, and meaning without a lecture about the formal elements of art. Everyone was able to learn, to know about these elements by simply looking at what was there and being invited to respond to what they saw. This is a kind of knowing that we don't even consider learning.

Reflection is a time-out from activity. It allows us just to be, not to do. When we paint, or teach—or do anything—and stop to step back and reflect, we create a rhythm of work and see, work and look, work and think, work and take in, work and cogitate—back and forth, and back and forth. We breathe in and then we breathe out. As with breathing, all "in" or all "out" does not make for healthy living.

Monitoring what happens inside us is an essential element of reflection. When something is right, we experi-

71

ence a shift inside and respond with an "ahhhhh," an inner experience of harmony. We might feel that what we have been doing is fun and gives us a feeling of excitement and delight, a feeling of wholeness and completeness. Or, sensing that something is not quite right, we might sense a feeling of discomfort, as when our clothes do not fit right. Then we need to search for what is missing by making different choices than the ones we have made.

What might happen if we began to cultivate the attitude of reflection and experiment with it in our teaching? If we reflected on whatever we do—really took time out to observe plainly just what is there, to notice our feelings and ask ourselves what we would like to change—we would constantly present ourselves with opportunities for growth. We could begin reflecting on what we teach and how we are teaching it. We could discover what we like and what we do not.

It can be scary to stop and just see what is there and how we feel about it. We might find we need to change something.

In some ways, it is more "comfortable" not to stop to look or listen or reflect, to avoid the possible feeling of discomfort. But the discovery is worth the pain. We honor ourselves when we take time to reflect on what we do and how we feel about it.

And if we have the courage to do that, we can expect our awareness of the teaching process to expand and the students who benefit from our reflections to gain from our efforts. They, in turn, can be encouraged to pause and find space for themselves to take a long, deep breath and another look at themselves and their work. More than a chore to accomplish, reflection simply takes the willingness

72

to stop and the focus to step back and look and listen.

Teaching from the Inside Out

Some years ago I heard a quote attributed to the Buddha: "We do not learn by experience but by our capacity for experience." I stuck that quote away in a collection of quotes that I use to inspire adult students when I teach drawing. Each time I bring it out and talk about it, it seems my understanding of it widens. The idea that we all have an infinite capacity to take in—to absorb, to be present, to see more—inspires me.

There is something about simply being with a particular moment, a particular feeling, that allows us to expand. Imagine drawing a broccoli, for example. Your hand and eye connect with each tiny valley, each tiny hill of the broccoli. You are present and alive and respectful to its form, its unique shapes. When you do this, it is like seeing a broccoli for the very first time. You do not say, "Yeah, broccoli, I know broccoli, I've eaten broccoli twice a week for my whole life." You begin to experience this piece of broccoli as the most magnificent, incredible, living thing you have ever seen.

Each time we become engaged in seeing the shapes of things, we increase our capacity for experience. When we take in—by drawing or touching or smelling or listening—noticing fully what is there, we SEE. Our capacity widens. As we practice this very simple task of noticing what is right there, we realize that our capacity for experiencing is endless.

This capacity allows us to know more about ourselves, to become more sensitive to our own situation. We can then develop as teachers, as human beings, offering ourselves to young people who need our capacity for experi-

73

encing as much as they need any core curriculum. It is this growth, this capacity for experience that nurtures the eight attitudes outlined in this chapter.

When we apply these attitudes to our teaching, it becomes a process, an art form. When what manifests in the classroom comes from the inside, teaching is no longer a static, lock step, performance-oriented occupation. It becomes freed-up. The eight-fold path of teaching from the inside out produces flow and spontaneity.

When the classroom is treated like a canvas, the teacher (turned artist) creates compositions that come from her intuition. What is produced in the classroom bears her interests, her color, her line, and her form. Sometimes, as with literal paint on literal canvas, the out-come does not meet her expectations. Other times, there is clarity and rhythm and balance, and everyone involved is moved to learn thoroughly—both experientially and conceptually. And always, the classroom is alive because it demands all the participants to live each moment as it unfolds.

For this to happen, everyone—teacher and children—needs to be SENSITIVE, to have COURAGE, to allow NOT-KNOWING and insecurity, to RISK feeling foolish at times, to LISTEN to each other and pay close ATTEN-TION to the process as it unfolds, and, perhaps most importantly, to TRUST in the process and take time to REFLECT.

PRACTICES

Sensitivity

1) Do you take time for yourself every day? If you do, how do you spend it? In your journal, write about how

this time is valuable to you. If you do not take personal time, consider why not. In your journal, list your reasons. Write about how such time would be of value to you.

2) Practice being more aware of the five senses. Take time to look, to listen, to touch, to taste (without talking or reading, with your eyes closed), to smell. As a daily exercise, select one of the senses and spend five minutes focusing on it. Write down what you discovered. How could you help your students be more aware of their senses?

Courage

1) Is it difficult for you to be yourself, even if you meet with disapproval? Journal about what happens to your creativity when you do something to please others. In what ways could you change this?

Not Knowing

1) Think of a time in your classroom when you did not understand what was happening or know the answer. How did you feel about it? What did you do? Did you tell anyone you did not understand or know or did you pretend that you did? Write in your journal about this experience.

2) When you allow your students to express their unique gifts by discovering the best way for each to express herself, what happens? Describe this in your journal.

Risk

1) Think about a time in your classroom when you were anxious about what was going to happen. How did

you handle it? Write in your journal about your reactions. What can you learn from this?

2) What do you do when you have a spontaneous idea?

3) What does taking risks add to your life?

4) Imagine doing something risky. Create a specific "chancy" situation in your mind. In your journal, write down what you imagine might happen, what your feelings might be.

Listening

1) Do you feel listened to most of the time, some of the time, little of the time, none of the time? With whom do you feel the most heard? Describe in your journal what that is like. With whom do you feel the least heard? Describe in your journal what that is like.

2) Describe in your journal your ability to listen to other people. What keeps you from listening empathetically? What helps you listen carefully?

3) Practice listening. Stop for several moments wherever you are and just listen. Write in your journal everything you hear—from the sounds farthest away, to those that are nearby, to those inside yourself.

4) Practice being totally present when someone talks to you. Practice listening not only to their words but to their body language and ask yourself if their body posture is consistent with what they are saying. Can you hear what the person is really communicating by listening to

both their words and observing their posture? Describe in your journal how this helps you understand what they are saying.

5) Connect your discoveries about listening to how you listen to your students. Journal your thoughts and feelings.

Attention

1) Sit down, close your eyes, and scan your body from head to toe. What do you experience? Are there any tight places? Write in your journal about your experience.

2) Find something you love to look at and spend at least five minutes paying attention to all its facets. Draw it in your journal. What is your experience? Write your observations in your journal.

3) Examine your curriculum with focus, as if you are looking at it through a microscope. What do you see? Write down in your journal what is there without evaluating it. Simply pay attention and see what is there.

Trust

1) Consider your level of trust in others and in yourself. Is there anything you want to change? If so, write in your journal about this.

2) Write down those activities in which you feel confident. Write down those activities in which you feel insecure. Look at both lists and refer to them from time to time to see if some activities move from the insecure column to the confident column. Note this information in your journal.

77

Reflection

1) Think about the times during a typical day in which reflection is built into your activity, such as when looking in a mirror while dressing. Journal about what this kind of reflection does for you.

2) Think about an activity that you know you will be doing with your students tomorrow and plan a period of reflection to add to it. Ask your students: How do you feel about it? What did you like? What could be improved? Write in your journal about the information you glean from this. Write down some ways you could use this information to alter that activity when you choose to do it again.

Teaching from the Inside Out

1) When have you felt that your capacity for experience has expanded? What were the circumstances? Reflect and write in your journal about these experiences.

Savoring
the Moments

What's in a Moment?

When we care deeply about children's and teachers' development, but cannot change the political realities of the school systems soon enough, we can begin where we are, in this moment, and see where it might take us.

Moments, each one pregnant with possibilities, can draw us away from daily problems and attendant discouragement and turn our attention to the present. In the present is everything. Listening to the heartbeat of any situation, to its rhythm, and realizing our connectedness to it helps us uncover the nugget of creativity embedded in each situation and, most importantly, within ourselves. It takes practice. It calls on all of the attitudes of the eight-fold path to making art and learning meaningful and memorable: sensitivity, courage, not-knowing, risk, listening, attention, trust and reflection.

If we know from our own experience that life's solutions do not come from trying to control situations but, instead, from paying close attention to what is happening in front of our noses, we already know that information and inspiration for the next move will emerge. Life is abundant and will yield its fruits.

William Carlos Williams, a doctor who loved practicing medicine, and a poet who used "the humdrum, day-in, day-out, everyday work" of being a doctor as inspiration for his poetry, offers some useful advice from his active life:

> "The thing isn't to find the time for
> it—we waste hours everyday doing
> absolutely nothing at all—the difficulty is
> to catch the evasive life of the thing . . .
> [which] will yield a moment of insight . . .
> We are lucky when that underground cur-
> rent can be tapped and the secret spring of
> all our lives will send up its pure water."

I have been fortunate enough to be a part of many wonderful moments in some schools when that "secret spring" seemed to be bubbling. They have been moments whose inspiration swept us—children, teacher and me— into a creative, joyous, perplexing, exciting, and meaningful journey into learning. I invite you to come into the classroom with me to share a few of these moments.

Following Our Dreams

My initial visit with Kristin took place in her classroom in an overcrowded school on the southwest side of Chicago. The classroom, like Kristin herself, was cheery and bright with sunlight, reflecting the kind of work that she was doing as a teacher. There were stories that the children had written hanging on the wall and drawings accompanied many of them. Through the windows you could see Holy Cross, the huge Catholic Church that was the center of this predominantly Mexican neighborhood. Kristin's classroom, like many others, was across the street from the school building because the population in the area had grown so large that alternative spaces had to be found.

Kristin taught in a federally-funded program. The students who came to her room were "pulled out" of their regular classrooms because they had been identified as "slow learners." They were below grade level, largely because of poor English language skills, owing to the fact that their first language was Spanish, the language in which they still felt and thought. Kristin wanted to help the children expand their English vocabulary. There was money available from the government for "enrichment," a term loosely used to bring artists into the school to offer alternative approaches to help the children with their learning difficulties. That was why I was there. I was part of The Children's Literacy Project from National Lewis University, and the arts were to be a conduit for the children's learning. I was to model using the arts in the curriculum.

I could see very quickly that we needed to find a way to increase the children's self-esteem. Then, their vocabulary would increase naturally. I was warmed by Kristin's open manner as soon as I meet her, and I was eager to dis-

81

cover how we might work together. As we talked back and forth that first morning, I invited Kristin to tell me about her own interests and what she really wanted from me. In these fragile first moments, we were two people finding their unique way of creating a partnership. Kristin revealed that she was currently reading one of her favorite stories, Raold Dahl's "James and the Giant Peach," to the children, As she spoke, I remembered loving that story, too, when I had read it to my own children. It is a story full of fantastic images, in particular a giant peach that becomes a home for a cast of animal characters and the main character, James. We both connected with this story, and Kristin told me that the children loved it, too. Why not begin there?

We started brainstorming about how we could use the story. Building on the fantasy aspect, we could talk with the children about fantasy and contrast that with reality. We could, couldn't we, ask the children to design a fantastic place, using the giant peach as inspiration? I suggested that clay might be a wonderful medium to use. Its nature is expressive and yielding, and it is ideal for children who have trouble expressing themselves verbally. Kristin liked this idea and told me there was an old, old kiln on the third floor of the school building that was never used. In fact, only one teacher even knew how to use it. (Pity, I thought. Everyone could be making and firing clay objects.) Kristin volunteered to ask this teacher if we could fire some clay pieces.

We had arrived at our starting place. I went home to re-read "James and the Giant Peach" and see what else it stirred in me. We were both excited.

Everything changed that first session in the classroom. After getting acquainted with the children, we began where we had planned, discussing James and his giant peach. I asked the children if they thought this was a real story.

"Nooooooooooo," they laughed.

"What then?" I asked.

I wrote F A N T A S Y large on the blackboard. Then I wrote R E A L I T Y next to it.

"What's real?" I asked.

"We are. The buildings are."

"The peach?"

They decided the peach was not.

"Then the peach must be fantastic?"

"Yes, yes!"

"Well, then, what is `fantastic'?"

"Halloween is. Dreams are."

Ahhhhhhh, dreams. I had a sudden sense that we ought to go down this avenue and see what was there.

"Let's talk about dreams," I found myself saying, knowing we were definitely going down an alternative path to the one we had chosen. I looked over to Kristin and silently asked her if we could take this diversion, not knowing where it might lead. She nodded and we were off. We began talking about dreams, about how anything can happen in them; how people can walk through walls; how we can be princes, demons, or frogs; how we can feel over-joyed, perplexed, or frightened. I invited the children to remember a dream, maybe the one that they had last night or maybe a recurring dream.

There was silence.

They were listening and reflecting and calling up their images. Fearing that it might be hard for them to talk about their dreams, I offered one from my own childhood about a sandman who would not let me go unless I

83

reached the light. Only then would he disappear.

My offering helped. The children raised their hands and began spilling out their fantastic tales. Their words were hard to understand. Their English was not extensive enough for what they wanted to express, and there was not enough time left for everyone to talk.

"Write them down," I suggested. Some of the children were eager, but I sensed this was going to be difficult for others. "You can draw your dream if you'd rather. Either way is okay."

It was time for me to go.

I felt excited as I walked down the stairs after that class. I knew we were on to something that could be both delightful and risky. Would the children be able to talk about their dreams, these intimate and revealing inner tales? And if they could, would these powerful stories lead them, with renewed interest, into broadening not only their vocabulary but also their images of themselves? Would we be able to follow what had emerged unplanned and see where it would take us? Was Kristin set on doing the fantastic clay project or would she be able to go in this new direction? I would not know until I returned to the class the following week.

When I walked into the classroom the next Tuesday, the children had delighted expressions on their faces. I could hardly wait to hear and see what had transpired during the week. Kristin handed me a stack of papers as she told me that the children had actually written their dreams. I was thrilled. I began to read aloud one dream after the other. They were wonderful, clearly expressed, and full of intimate detail.

"I dreamed that I was in space and it was real dark and I saw other planets."

"Genero thought that a boogeyman was coming out of his lunch . . . His eyes were as big as a potato."

"Once I was dreaming me and my sister lived in a far-away kingdom. We were so rich that we had a lot of clothes and a big house. . . . Then I woke up. I turned the lights on and I wasn't rich anymore."

One little girl told about her father dying and how he was lonely and wanted her to come with him to heaven.

I was amazed and touched by the revelation of so many inner aches and their wishes for an altogether different existence. The children's honesty moved me . . . and they knew it. Their telling their dreams, Kristin's help and support in that process, and my reading the dreams aloud seemed to bond us in a special way. Our inner lives did not have to be so secret. We could talk about them, even write about them. Next, we would draw them.

After class Kristin and I talked. She was as thrilled as I about what the children had written, so we decided to abandon our original plans for the fantastic clay pieces and continue down this dream path to see where it would lead. She was able to tolerate the anxiety that "not-knowing" produces and risk the outcome. We were working together as partners and were able to support each other in this process.

Time flew by as the children wrote, re-wrote, and drew their dreams. But their drawing lacked something: The images were undefined and not nearly as interesting as the children's written versions. I could sense their discouragement and my own as well. Here was a moment all too familiar to artists in the process of creating. It is a time of doubting what you are doing. I wondered how to

85

proceed, how to help the children over this seeming impasse.

I reflected on the drawings with the children, offering gentle critique: "Be more specific. What did the monster under your bed look like? What were his teeth like, his eyes, hair, hands, feet? What expression, what color? Or, was the hand that slapped you big or small?" If there were several parts to the dream, I encouraged the children to draw them all, calling up every image they could, reassuring them that somehow we would put them all together. They zeroed in. Kristin and I zeroed in. We were all dedicated to this moment-by-moment process of making each image as full as possible.

As I looked at the writing and re-read the dreams aloud to the class from time to time, I realized that the simple sentences the children were using were more poetry than prose. I saw that the written material could be in free poetic form and be put together with the drawings in such a way that each would enhance the other, yet be a single creative expression. I did not want the drawings to be illustrative, nor did I want the writing to explain the drawings. Instead, I envisioned the writing and the drawing becoming a single seamless work of art. To do this would mean that the words on the page would have to be as artful as the drawings. The words would have to adhere to the rubrics of visual expression, that is, they would have to have line, form, composition, and be fitted into the drawings in such a way that each would compliment the other.

Words are usually thought of as only vehicles for the message. We would have to stretch our concept of words-as-messages into words-as-shapes as well. We would need to look at each letter as a shape and also see how each letter-shape related to the other. I encouraged the children to think about the letter "G" as a curve and straight line. What would it look like next to an "E"—all straight lines, three horizontal and one vertical? And what about shaping letters in such a way to express the meaning of a word? "Wave," for example, could be written one letter up and the next down to resemble a wave. Or "monster" could be written real small to express the terror one feels calling monster images to mind. Or the words of the dream/poem "me slapping my boyfriend outside my house everyday" might go around a big hand. The words of the poem from a child who "was dreaming that in Chicago there was going to come a big monster in every house" could be written within the monster itself.

This idea of words-as-shapes added a new dimension to the creative process and a new challenge. The children loved it. Our concepts of writing, drawing, symbols, shapes were being stretched. We were in unfamiliar territory, but because we explored this new ground step-by-step, it was solid. Everyone was riveted to each new phase as this dream project unfolded.

Finally, after working separately at creating letters as shapes and adding the visual elements of the dreams, we were ready to put it all together. As the children completed their compositions, everything seemed to fall into place. They were ready for color and were eager to use brand new Magic Markers to refine and bring nuance to their picture-poems.

They plunged in eagerly, exploring color. They were excited about what they had worked so hard to create and seemed to rush ahead to complete this many-faceted project. Whoa, I thought. What we need right now is a reflection, a critique. This urgency to be finished was one I was all too familiar with. When I am unable to be focused, I rush from one moment to the next. Children are also victims of this "rush ahead" disease. I knew it was important at that moment to make space, to take a long deep breath, so that everyone could step back and see where they had come from and where they were going.

We took an entire class period for our reflection on the work in progress. Kristin and I tacked all the drawings on the board. Wow! Was it a charge to see what everyone had done and for each kid to have her or his work looked at by classmates! Before we started our critique, I reminded the children that critiquing did not mean criticizing and tearing apart. It meant, instead, to see what we liked best and to also see what might be changed to make it better. We looked at each picture-poem intensely and examined it, each child talking about the picture-poem first and the rest of us giving feedback. The children were inspired by having their work noticed so appreciatively, and they returned to finish their work with renewed attention and focus.

The creation of these picture-poems was truly a delight. The gradual blossoming of this project kept us all on our toes, examining each step as we were doing it. Our focus on each moment helped us uncover new possibilities inherent in each stage of the project. By staying close to each of these moments, it became clear what the next step would be. In looking back, of course, we could see how successfully the development took place. However, being with each step as it evolved kept us all in a state of questioning, wondering. How would it be? Would we be able to be expressive, to tell our stories, to draw them, to think about words and letters visually, to integrate words and images in such a way as to make them work together? We did not know; all we knew was that we were having the time of our lives doing it. The result: work that was beautiful, clear, unusual; work that was a vehicle for the children to expand their self-esteem and their English vocabulary. We were all able to tap into the "silent spring" of our lives that yielded our bubbling energy that could not be hidden.

Finding Out Where We Are

Why is it that we always want to be somewhere other than where we are?

Most of my life I thought that living any place but Chicago would fill my soul. I certainly could not be content in Chicago. After all, Chicago was flat, bounded on three sides by cement, and I needed to be in the East (or the West) where there were hills and trees—a surprise around every corner. Happiness, excitement, adventure surely could not be found here, where I was.

One day my husband, who was involved in helping restore the few remnants of prairie around Chicago, took me to see a huge track of undisturbed prairie about two hours from Chicago. It was June. The purple prairie cone flower was in bloom, a pinkish daisy-like blossom with a raised gum-drop like center, standing three feet tall on a sturdy, thick stalk. When we arrived that warm June afternoon, having driven down dusty roads looking for this hidden piece of genuine Illinois prairie, we were both excited. When we stood on this land that had been prairie for thousands of years, I was thrilled as I looked at the sight before me. Thousands of cone flowers waved lightly in the breeze. I felt as though I were looking at a pink ocean, heaving and rolling beneath a blue sky. With my feet planted on this land, I understood living in a prairie

89

state. I felt "at home" in the Midwest for the first time in my life.

So, when Paula, a teacher in an overcrowded inner city school, told me—without much enthusiasm—that her fourth-grade students had been studying the grasslands of the world and that she planned on doing a project about the Australian grasslands, I blurted out, "Australia! Why not study our own native grasslands, the Illinois prairie— what was once right beneath our feet?"

Paula looked at me questioningly, so I continued. "If we studied the Illinois prairie, the children could have a feel for their own land. They could imagine arriving on the shores of Lake Michigan, looking west as far as the eye could see through native tall grasses and flowers, no buildings and trees to block the view. If the children could get to know and love their own land, they might feel less alienated from where they live—and from themselves."

Paula was interested but somewhat reluctant to give up the mural of Australian grasslands she had wanted. We are so accustomed to thinking that important knowledge issues from places long ago and far away! We have also been taught that information comes in books or curricula fashioned by "experts." What we are not so aware of is that a collection of "facts" (unrelated to our lives) also tend to keep interest and feeling at arm's length.

"I guess it could be the Illinois prairie," Paula mused. "Why not?" She tentatively took the first step of risk, willing to go beyond "the facts." She confessed she did not know much about the prairie. I might not either, had I not had access, through my husband, to information we could work from.

This was Paula's first year teaching in the public schools, but she brought ten years experience from the

90

Catholic schools. She was conscientious, calm, and organized. We talked in the women's bathroom across the hall from her classroom, the only place in this overcrowded school that we could have a private conversation.

As Paula and I talked, pictures began to form in my mind of brightly painted prairie plants cut out of plywood. I envisioned them standing up (somehow), forming a "wooden prairie" that could be moved around, creating various compositions. We could, if we wanted, walk through it, among the sculptures. I could not hold back my enthusiasm and the ideas it engendered. If Paula really wanted to do an Australian mural after I explained my ideas, we would do it. But at least she would have a choice.

I described what I could see in my mind's eye: a charming wooden prairie created by nine-year-olds. We could, I suggested, enlarge botanical drawings of individual prairie plants to make it easy for the children to draw them. This would help them know the plants individually, and drawing is such an excellent tool for learning to observe how something is put together. They could learn their names and begin to appreciate these plants from our native environment. Each child could then choose the plant she or he liked best and enlarge it, creating a template for sketching it on plywood. And finally, I would bring in my jigsaw so we could cut out the enlarged drawings from plywood. Then we could paint them.

I paused. Paula was delighted and, although my plan would require a major time commitment, she wanted to do it. She was interested in where I got this idea. Had it come to me full blown?

Paula was sensitive to what lay beneath our conversation, to the very formation of an idea. Her question

91

caused me to reflect a bit on where and how creative ideas
come into being. I was aware that I had a choice whether
to share my ideas as they came tumbling into my consciousness or to follow Paula's lead and go along with
doing a mural of Australian grasslands. Taking the risk to
share my creative pulse and see where it went grew out of
my own experience of using a jigsaw to create large wood-
en sculptures of people—and out of my enthusiasm for
the prairie. I had taken a risk by expressing my ideas and
I hoped that my example would inspire Paula to honor
and express hers—and be an artful teacher.

   With both of us riding the wave of our, now, mutual
excitement, we talked about various prairie possibilities.
Paula's suggestions poured out. What about a field trip to
the prairie in the spring? Maybe we could germinate and
grow prairie plants inside during the winter months.
Then we could see about starting a prairie in a vacant lot
in front of the school. We had our research cut out for us.
For our first session, we decided to tell the children about
our Illinois prairie tradition and how it got lost.

   As I started gathering resources, I found a book of
individual botanical drawings of prairie plants of Illinois. I
poured through the book, identifying the ones whose
shapes were definite and easy to remember and then
enlarged them on a photocopier. I called a prairie nursery
to find out about planting seeds in the classroom and discovered that prairie plants need a controlled environment
and take a longer time to germinate than we had. But we
could plant sunflower seeds—a cousin of the prairie vari-
ety—that would grow easily within a classroom setting. I
ordered a little-known book, sold by an historic site near
the prairie my husband and I had visited, that had a history and beautiful photographs of the original Illinois

prairie. I borrowed slides of prairie plants to show the class. I was counting on these multiple modes of acquiring knowledge to increase the children's appreciation of the common prairie ecology and to inspire their creativity.

During that first session, we pictured in our minds the various Native American tribes—the Illinois, Potawatamie, Kickapoo, and Miami—roaming through the tall grasses hunting bison on the land where we now live, what we now know as Chicago. We let ourselves experience what the first colonists might have felt when, after knowing only hills and forests, they suddenly saw a flat and limitless field of tall grasses the height of grown men and women. We talked about those first settlers probably not even realizing they had discovered land with the richest soil in the world, land that could also be used for sod houses because of the tangle, sturdiness, and depth of the prairie root system. We felt like pioneers, imagining ourselves as the new settlers trying to find comfort from a land that felt foreign. We pictured the prairie as it once was, two-hundred years ago, covering the entire state of Illinois. We understood that, through farming, the prairie has largely been destroyed and, until recently, all but forgotten.

It was January when we

93

began this project, so we couldn't actually experience a real prairie until spring. However, we could imagine this land and see pictures of how it looked. I showed slides of prairie landscapes—the broad sweep—as well as close-ups of individual prairie plants. The mixture of grasses and flowers created a soft prairie bouquet and invited the children to experience the loveliness of this landscape. At the end of the first session, I passed out the enlarged botanical drawings of individual prairie plants. The children each choose one to use for their own drawings of the plants.

"Look at your plant carefully before you start," I told them. "Feel how the stem grows, see how the leaves attach to the stem, where the flowers come from." I wanted them to observe, to go slowly, becoming attentive to detail. I wanted them to experience that drawing is observation and that kind of investigation is research: children become scientists while drawing and exploring something for the first time. I wanted them to become familiar enough with the various plant forms so they could name them as they went along.

In order to diminish their anxiety, I gave them only simple materials at first: pencils and plain white typing paper. If we had used art materials, the materials could easily have become the focus of attention, so we shelved them until the children had practice learning to look and draw how a plant grows. We encouraged the children to select as many different botanical plant drawings as they wanted. They dove in, and it became a game: They would choose one, draw it, and then select another.

When I returned the following week, the children were eager to show me the drawings they had done during the week. It was clear that having a "personal" botanical plant picture to draw from was important. Paula was as proud of the work as her students. I was impressed with their observational skills. I could see in their drawings that many of them had been able to see how the plant was formed. These were no cookie-cutter drawings of plants. The children had studied the plants carefully as they were learning how to let their eyes and hands work together.

"Drawing gives us information," I told them. "It helps us see better, become focused, and notice the world around us. When we sit still and look intently, we become more aware and begin to see the beauty in a small object. Drawing is also communication," I added, "because when you draw, you tell what you see."

I suggested that they continue drawing the plants, this time concentrating on seeing the actual shapes—each leaf, each stem—for what it was, not for what they thought a leaf or a stem ought to look like. "Labeling," I explained, "which is what we do when we determine, 'That this is a leaf, and I know what a leaf is,' keeps us from drawing the shape of things. We draw what we know, not what we see.

95

"Focus on each petal of a blossom," I continued. "Each shape in nature is totally unique, "and in order to see it for what it is, we must be careful to draw its special-ness. Plants are really no different than people. We can recognize a person, but knowing details about that per-son—height, color of eyes, hair, personality—helps us appreciate each one as unique."

As the children continued exploring the terrain of their plant, their eyes became more attuned to nuances. Paula helped the children plant sunflower seeds and create an exhibit of prairie materials with posters and drawings of the prairie, watercolors of mine, and many books that formed a "prairie library." As a class, the chil-dren were becoming immersed in original Illinois land-scape.

It was time for the children to look through all their drawings and choose the one they liked best. This practice in discrimination was an exercise in reflection that would help them learn to make choices. Each child then drew her or his favorite plant on large sheets of brown wrap-ping paper. Being expert drawers by now, this was simple.

Then came the moment the kids had been waiting for. I brought in my jigsaw and several sheets of one-quarter-inch plywood. When I plugged in the jigsaw and held the trigger, they could hear the roar. They were definitely impressed. The roar had gotten their attention so com-pletely, I had no trouble telling them how careful they had to be while using it!

I love the opportunity to use power tools with children because it empowers them. I believe that when we allow children to use a power tool, we show our respect for them by treating them as responsible people. And respect helps raise their self-esteem, a much-needed quality in desperately low quantity, especially in our inner city schools.

Our "prairie" classroom became a workshop, filled with activity. We plugged in the jigsaw and the cutting began! While some children were cutting out their prairie plants (with an adult assistant for security), other children were coloring their brown-wrapping paper pieces with delicious colors using oil sticks to begin the process of discovering the colors they would eventually use when they painted their wooden pieces.

As we all launched into the painting of the project, the room became alive with energy. Numerous shades of greens were mixed and used to create a basically green prairie, but it was freely dotted with splashes of purple, yellow, and red. Details were added: shades of other greens in patterns or tone, outlines around flowers or leaves. The sculptures were enchanting.

There is always a time at the end of a project when everyone is ready to be finished, even if there is more that could be done. It is a time that must be addressed or the project ends with a whimper instead of a bang. The excitement of cutting and painting was completed. Now what? We looked at pieces informally, reflecting on what we saw. The consensus was that it was time to put the sculptures together in some fashion.

For the next session, I brought in four-by-eight

97

wooden stands with slots in them that Paula and I handed out. As each child carefully fitted her or his sculpture into the grooves so it would stand alone, they grew more and more excited. The sculptures looked magnificent standing on their own, appearing as if they were sprouting right out of the children's desks. I invited the children to bring their pieces to the front of the room and to stand them wherever they wished. Suddenly the sculptures became an instant wooden garden, shapes intermingling together to create other shapes, and colors more vibrant together than alone. We were all amazed at how beautiful they looked together.

During my final session in the classroom, we took pictures of the children in our "prairie garden." Two or three children knelt or sat on the floor, peeking through some of the leaves. They were participants now in the garden, not simply observers of their individual pieces.

But this project did not end within the classroom. Even before we completed our sculptures, I could see how imaginative they were going to be, so I had contacted the Chicago Botanic Garden to see if we could display our "prairie garden" there. The director loved the idea, and an exhibit date was scheduled for shortly before school would be out, a time when some of the prairie plants in the Botanic Gardens would be in bloom. We arranged a field trip both to see our wooden prairie plants and the actual ones.

When childrens' artwork goes beyond the classroom, learning is raised to a different level. Public display validates learning through the visual and makes it an important part of the child's life. It is a thrill for children to see that someone cares enough about what they have made to honor it by exhibiting it. An exhibit announces the artist's depth of understanding and creativity. The self-esteem value of a public exhibit is inestimable.

Exhibiting children's artwork also becomes a teaching tool for the viewer. The freshness and guilelessness of children's artwork refreshes the spirit. Other children and adults learn about the range of perspectives that people have when considering the same subject.

For this fourth-grade class, seeing their sculptures in a public space was inspiring. The children darted around the exhibition space each trying to find his or her own piece. On the stand was their name and the plant that their piece represented. They stood in front of their pieces, fascinated and noticeably proud of their work and its appearance in this great public gallery. After admiring their sculptures, we all went to the gardens to see the real prairie plants. There they were: Spiderwort, Prairie Dock, Compas Plant. Immediately the children named them like old friends. The children had become intimate with them through the process of drawing and drawing and drawing and naming and enlarging and cutting out and painting their wooden prairie plants.

During this project, we had pushed ourselves to the edge of our competence while inventing what we did as we went along. I dared to speak about my fantasy to a teacher I had just met. Paula dared to participate fully, learning each skill and extending the learning into her curriculum. The children dared to look and to continue looking while they drew the intimate details of the plants. We all dared to use a power tool without the usual attendant fear that someone would lose a finger to keep us from doing it. We stood on the edge, continually pushing back our ignorance. And we all learned that by continuing our step-by-step process, we would arrive where we needed to be—right at home on the Illinois prairie.

Uncovering Mysteries

Yolanda and I had worked together before. We had both been involved in a three-year project in which three arts people contributed time and expertise in two Chicago public schools.

During the last year of the project, the teachers and arts people decided to select an overall theme that would allow each class to study a different corner of the universe while, at the same time, tying into a larger theme that would bring us all together as a cohesive group. One morning, everyone sat together, pushing away their separate agendas and concerns, and we came up with a broad theme that everyone could connect to: cultures around the world.

Yolanda told me that she wanted to do something on the Aborigines of Australia, about whom I knew nothing. Neither did she, but she wanted to learn. I got a large and beautiful book on Aboriginal art at the library and began to familiarize myself with it, drinking in the beauty of this magical art form. The paintings were abstract and mystical, simple and readable. They looked like a code that told a story. I read about the Aborigine's "Dreamings," their stories that told of the beginning of things, connecting the present to the past. I found it difficult to understand their cosmology, so I turned to the stories themselves. They eluded me, but I could see in them that the Aborigine's way of looking at the world was different from ours. They see that everything is connected and they view every piece of the world with respect because it all springs from the same divine origin. Everything they touch isn't merely a

100

separate object but is interrelated. Everything is alive. How could Yolanda and I make this unspeakable feeling understandable and "felt" for sixth grade, practical kids?

We had developed an easy relationship over the two years of our project together, so I felt safe in not-knowing—acknowledging that I was struggling to grasp Aboriginal culture. The day we began the project, I told the kids and Yolanda that I did not comprehend this ancient culture and how it worked, but that I would tell them what I did understand. I felt liberated by speaking honestly and not pretending to be an expert.

We started by looking at reproductions of Aborigine paintings.

"Everything in these paintings has meaning," I told the class. "There is not a color or a mark that doesn't in some way reflect the story the artist is trying to tell. This is a code, and you can use it to paint a story."

I left some of the stories and the book of paintings for everyone to look at. When I returned, the kids had read many of the stories and looked at the paintings. They had even taken the Aborigine stories and used them as inspiration to write their own. Their stories, actually compilations of the original and the children's creative additions, were Aborigine-like stories. The kids had somehow found their way inside the spirit of the "Dreamings."

The next step in understanding was to create symbols for these stories that could be used for their own paintings. During the week, the children learned some of the Aborigine symbols and created others that they needed in order to tell their own "Dreamings."

Yolanda and I decided that it would be good for the kids to work together in groups. That way, the ones with the strongest imagery and understanding could help and inspire the others in the group. Each group of five or six gathered to write one story from their individual ones. Singly, each child drew a personal version of the story. Then, together, they selected elements from each of the drawings to make a composite group painting that represented every child's ideas.

We pushed a group of desks together to create a spacious surface, one that would take a large piece of butcher paper. The paper was sturdy and covered the space, allowing the children to group around the paper. The kids worked together beautifully. They sat in their groups dis-

cussing color and composition: which color to use or how to compose their collaborative painting. They talked and painted, the rhythm easily alternating back and forth. They inspired one another. When one was stuck, another helped. The children with the weakest self-esteem were uplifted by those who were more confident. What they wove together reflected their cohesiveness. My role, after initially exposing the children to Aborigine art and dreamings, was simply to support the work that was unfolding. As the weeks went by, these paintings evolved into colorful, clear abstract paintings.

The paintings emerged, each divided into sections with animals, insects, and markings interpreting the stories the children had written. The designs seemed to

102

spring from a knowing about how stories and symbols complement one another. The drawings were inventive and beautiful and did not need explaining. They truly represented the spirit of Aborigine art. I was amazed that these children had so quickly picked up on this Aboriginal material and interpreted it with the ease of the initiated. What had begun as a real mystery and a seeming block to understanding turned out to stimulate the children to discover the underbelly of this wonderful artform.

Another rewarding dimension of this project was the partnership that Yolanda and I formed during the three years we worked together. As trust developed between us, we were able to support one another while we creatively explored this exciting and mysterious culture, thus making it accessible to children.

Yolanda's easy-going style was a lesson for me. My confusion about the meaning of the "Dreamings" did not phase her a bit. She simply plowed on, one foot in front of the other, and the children followed. We started by looking, really looking, at the Aboriginal paintings. Together, we unmasked the symbols. Then came the stories. If we did not understand them, we simply composed endings to the stories that satisfied us. We developed our own code from our compiled Aborigine-student stories, and we embedded the codes in our drawings on paper. There was magic in this process. What had seemed like an obstacle to me became an opportunity for us to use our creative energies to understand the mysterious. In this way, we kept the spirit of this spirited culture and studied a remote people and their energy-filled universe.

The three-year project came to completion at the end of that academic year. The artwork that poured in from our collective theme of "cultures around the world" was outstanding, and I wanted to bring all the parts together in some fashion. The children in the separate classrooms in the two schools, I reasoned, would be able to broaden their horizons even more by seeing the work exhibited together. And teachers and administrators from the schools could see the value of understanding cultures by making art.

The education department at the Terra Museum of American Art in Chicago gave us space to exhibit the artwork for one week. The paintings, hangings, and sculptures were hung and installed. We created a catalog explaining the project and each of the cultures that the classrooms studied. Each piece was labeled with the child's name, classroom, and school. The walls sparkled with the children's artwork. Walking through the exhibit gave the viewer a sense of the different cultures— England, Japan, Africa, India, Aboriginal Australia—as the children saw them.

The exhibit provided a visual forum for viewing and discussing the work in a context separate from the classroom. Yolanda and her sixth graders were deservedly proud of their contribution. They had cracked Aboriginal dream-time, digested it, and told their experience of it through painting and writing, not a small accomplishment for eleven-year-olds.

Making the effort of mounting the exhibit was not only a way of celebrating the work we had done together for three years, but it also conveyed a larger meaning because all the work was displayed as a whole. As a group of teachers, children, and artists, we were able to see the unity throughout the varied cultures.

Watching each group of children gather around their own work and admire it made me aware of the unique

104

experience children have when adults honor them by honoring their work. I was also deeply aware that an exhibit like this tells others—parents, teachers, and administrators—how the arts make learning accessible and bring us to integration, allowing us to overcome the division between feeling and thought.

Making art brings deep satisfaction because it is part of our nature to express our learning and our experiences through color and movement and sound—and the many languages that are our birthright. Teaching from the inside out cultivates these languages and helps them to surface, while children who are guided by adults in touch with their expressive powers can't help but prosper. We must wake up to our many creative expressions and exercise them.

Making art makes us whole.

PRACTICES

Following Our Dreams

1) Think of a time when you did something different from what you had planned, a time when you saw something that interested, challenged, and excited you. What did you do? Did you do what you had prepared or did you create something from your interest? How did it turn out? Describe this experience in your journal. If you have never changed course in the middle of doing something, reflect on why not. Is it fear, anxiety, the feeling of not having enough time? Make notes of your thoughts in your journal.

Finding Out Where We Are

1) Take some time and discover more about the par-

ticular place in which you live. What has happened recently that has meaning for you and also relates to where you live? Note this in your journal.

2) Notice the plant life where you are. Take one of the plants and write about it in your journal for ten minutes without stopping. Do not worry about spelling or punctuation. Draw the plant, taking the time to notice its contour and texture. Add color (watercolor, colored pencils, etc.) Experiment by trying different media. How does this help you better know that plant? How might this be used in your classroom? Note your observations in your journal.

3) Think about the space in your classroom. Could you arrange space for a children's gallery, with frequent exhibitions of children's artwork? What would an exhibit need: A title? A catalog? Invitations sent to other classrooms? How could the children in your class participate: Designing the exhibit? Hanging the exhibit? As docents for other classes? What would you need to do to make this possible. Note your discoveries in your journal.

4) When you have a great idea about an activity that excites you, do you write it down, blurt it out, or keep it to yourself? Note in your journal what you do with ideas. Do you need or want to do something different? If so, what? Write about this in your journal.

Uncovering Mysteries

1) Find a myth that you like. Either write a new ending or add to the one that is there. Create symbols for the different elements of the story and arrange them on a piece of paper, creating a composition. Use color. When

106

the story is completed in a visual form, make a "key" to inform the viewer about each object. That way your picture can be "read" by others. Try this with your students. Put the pictures up and have the children "read" each others' stories.

* * * * *

Remember the reflective exercise at the beginning of this book? Please repeat the exercise, without referring to what you wrote earlier. Read and ponder the following paragraph. Write down your responses.

> Focus on your main goal in being an educator, the one that is your driving force. (Do not let others' expectations intrude.) Write it large in a simple sentence. Contemplate what your teaching would look like to make that goal a reality and write down your description.

Now retrieve your first responses from the place where you stored them. Compare what you wrote. Does your goal differ? In what way? How have your responses changed? Take some additional time now to journal about any ideas and feelings that come to you during this reflective process.

* * * * *

Art Facilitators:
The Artists Who Work
In Schools

Elsewhere in this book I have suggested that it would be wonderful if every school in America had an artist in it. What could that mean for schools? How could they be different from the way they are now?

An artist in every school would be able to work individually with teachers or with groups of teachers to support new, creative ways of working with their curriculum. The artist would be a catalyst for change by supporting and prodding teachers and helping to infuse the school environment with the creative energy it takes to continue to make changes.

Sounds good, but what kind of artist can do this kind of work? We don't have a model for what this might look like. Presently, there is no association of teaching artists who come together to discuss how to work with other teachers. There are only various arts and education organizations that have their own programs and philosophies for artists who work in schools. This section is an attempt to explore the artist's role for on-going teacher development and whole school change and what it might take for a professional artist to become an arts facilitator in order to become valuable to schools and multiple ways of learning.

Art Facilitation: A Philosophy and Process

Facilitation means "to make easy." It is a natural process. What facilitation is not is having the right answers. Instead, it means that we are with another human being who wants to learn in such a way that he can discover his own inspiration. This way of being with another requires acceptance of the person as they are, with their ideas, no matter what your opinion is. It takes an attitude of not-knowing and trusting, the ability to listen and pay attention – qualities that go against the system of bells and top-down pressures. When we facilitate, we affirm that everything contributes to learning. Every single thing becomes material to create with. Like a weaving, nothing is thrown out. What is there in the environment? Ideas from both teacher and artist, the curriculum, and student's interests can all be woven into material for further investigation and learning.

An art facilitator is like an orchestra leader – who sees the unique qualities of all the players and the different sounds that each makes. The facilitator then works to bring out the highest quality from each player.

110

Understanding that no two instruments make the same sound – that the violin must sound like a violin, a trumpet like a trumpet – the facilitator can learn to cherish the differences in each person, each teacher, each student. Each voice is unique and must be nurtured in order to be appreciated. The facilitator must be willing to hear individual hopes and passions, the actual tones of the players, even in the midst of conformity and pressures, in order to respectfully help the natural sounds of the instrument (be it teacher or student) to emerge and flourish.

Unlike many artist-in-residence programs, whose goal is to work with students, art facilitation is primarily to serve the teachers. We know that whatever changes teachers make will effect the students they teach as well. Teachers impact the lives of their students on an on-going basis, so we must begin with the teachers, trusting that as they develop more and more confidence in their own creativity, the students will too.

Art Facilitation: The Partnership

During the process of working together, a relationship develops between artist and teacher. It is crucial that in starting out working together that an artist approaches the teacher with respect for the teacher's knowledge and particular challenges. The artist is on the teacher's turf and must seek to understand the teacher's philosophy of education. The artist is a presence as well as being a skilled artist, and the kind of presence can help or hinder a teacher in risking to learn new ways of teaching. What art facilitation calls for is different than when artists come to schools to do a single performance, where the teacher is asked to be a recipient of entertainment and information. What this work requires is time for both

111

teacher and artist to come together to renew perceptions of what it means to be an artful teacher. This kind of process is unlike most six- or eight-week residences where the student is the focus and what is expected of the teacher is to follow along. More extended time is required for true arts facilitation because what we are interested in is deep and permanent change, not a patch-up job or one that is oriented for short-term goals, like testing. This is the long view, where there is time for trust to develop between teacher and artist – trust being a key ingredient for people to risk themselves, expand, and be their creative selves.

Uninterrupted time for planning for teachers and artists on an on-going basis is critical. This is difficult to achieve, but worth the effort. When people are pressured, relationships are compromised and effective planning is diminished. Both parties should be present without the days accumulated burdens effecting the process of relating and reflecting on the issues of how to create new ways of learning.

So, all the have-tos of when and how to teach what, those hardened school expectations, need to be acknowledged and at the same time addressed. The mutual trust expected for creating a meaningful learning environment, where learning can emerge naturally, must be a priority. Both artist and teacher might be able to deal with the realities of the school environment if they can believe in the basic premise that whole-body activities (which can include movement, drama, music, and visual arts) effect learning.

When a teacher and artist become partners in creating a new environment, they are at a place where they can each believe that they have more to bring to the situa-

112

tion than they imagined. The partnership grows out of a relationship in which both parties realize their own talents and strengths while they also honor the unique skills and talents that the other brings to the learning situation. One of the goals of the partnership is for both artist and teacher to involve themselves in a process that will open broader possibilities for each being their most creative selves. Another is that the teacher's ways of teaching is always being examined. Without being intrusive, the artist can help the process by asking questions that could make the kinds of teaching that is being practiced known. By examining what is known, the teacher can question whether to change what is being done, and in what ways. Whatever the teacher is interested in pursuing is material for the art facilitator to use to help bring new projects into being. The image that comes to mind is that these two people, often swimming against the tide of school expectations, are standing on the edge of a precipice, willing to take a transformative leap into the unknown.

The Art of Art Facilitation

It is always delightful to watch children at play. They take what is present and transform it for their own use. They do not see the world in fragments, and they are not fragmented. Everything is fair game. Life is to interact with, to engage in a dialog with, and to play with. Blankets strewn across chairs become houses. Books and record players get dragged in to help create a private environment in which adults are excluded. A whole life is imagined within this private space. Other childrens' games include shaping mud carefully by hand to become cookies or pancakes, taking a spoon and attaching bits of paper and tape to become animated puppets or dolls, picking up

113

sticks to become weapons, or finding boxes to become secret and special places for found objects.

In much the same way, the art of art facilitation is treating one's work as play. The art facilitator sees what is there, extends it and enhances it with ideas from teacher, student, or artist. The artist can then help the teacher question and reflect on what is possible to do. It is a process similar to pulling taffy, finding out how much it will stretch. The art facilitator becomes the catalyst for the stretch, who, at the same time is always working to honor and support the teacher so the teacher's confidence can grow.

The art of art facilitation is not simply about knowing the skill of your artform. It includes perceptive skills of noticing possibilities. The entire classroom is the canvas, the material that is present is what is used to fill that canvas with color, line, and form. The art is in the art of creative connecting of curriculum and art together so that there is a seamless whole. Then, tight and ordered boundaries of separate subjects can fade. The arts unify what concepts divide.

Facilitation is a mysterious process that can bring people to the edge of their competence, where play and risk become more familiar than denial and resistance. Sometimes it requires gently offering support, and sometimes it means pushing someone who is almost there – just one more step into the unknown, breaking free of old concepts. There are situations where facilitation becomes a high art. It calls for knowing when to demonstrate in the classroom; when to observe; when to teach; when to step back while the teacher offers information, explanation or directions; what materials to offer to bring; how often to meet with the teacher before or after school.

114

Like any creative process, the results of facilitation are always uncertain, like creativity in any form. As artists, we read, study, muse, sketch, risk, try out, take another direction, expose ourselves to new materials – always pushing against our own resistances for break-throughs into new perceptions and creations. As we do this over and over again, often without the success we are looking for, we discover something is slowly shifting.

Briefly, the art of art facilitation comprises the following points:

1) Listening to the teacher, what is said and what is perceived to be the teacher's underlying wishes;

2) Observation of the teacher's style of teaching and the teacher's relationship to the students;

3) Offering suggestions for alternative ways to explore the subject matter;

4) Instructing the teacher in the necessary skills to make a project happen;

5) Offering different kinds of materials, other than the usual tempera paints and crayons found in schools;

6) Modeling and demonstrating in the classroom;

7) Sharing perceptions on how the project is proceeding with the class;

8) Brainstorming how various skills and ideas can be used with other curriculum; and

9) Reflecting with the teacher on what is happening, both internally and externally.

Because facilitation is an art and not a formula, flexibility is important to function differently in different situations with different people. Becoming an art facilitator – like becoming an artist – requires the long-term view, the one in which flexibility takes precedence over rigidly planned projects. It means always being ready and willing to alter plans to fit situations to a particular moment that presents itself. Knowing that art comes from within must be imprinted on the facilitator's mind so that they can nurture and protect that process in others.

The projects are not the goal. The process is. The projects themselves can serve as a stimulus for a fluid process of connecting "this" with "that", of seeing possibilities everywhere. The goal of facilitation is transformation. The hope is for educators to be able to see more possibilities by creating different structures, different attitudes and by using and transforming everyday events and materials.

When Facilitation Works

Facilitation works when the teacher wants what the facilitator has to give. I once did a mural residency with an eighth grade teacher. He welcomed me immediately into his classroom: he was the host, I was his guest. Fred offered me coffee and introduced me to the class. Everyone was excited about what we would do together.

One day early in this residency, I noticed a stack of newspapers in the corner of the classroom. I was curious about what he did with them. He said that he loved the Chicago Tribune, had, in fact, ordered subscriptions for every child in his class. He also told me that although he understood that he ought to be following the prescribed curriculum, he loved to teach what was important to him. His interest in the newspapers had engendered all kinds of innovative ideas that he used in his classroom. Fred was open. He knew what he liked and was eager to try new things.

Our time together flowed from one thing to another. I would suggest how to proceed and he would offer his suggestions. Together, and with the enthusiastic children, we made a mural. First, I needed to know what the children were interested in so that we could find a theme for the mural. After brainstorming a list of subjects, we decided that transportation could be a theme that everyone wanted to explore. As we worked on the mural week after week, we continued to open up the theme of transportation to include images of feet and roller skates and scooters and stilts, as well as the more usual trains, planes, cars, and bikes.

It was the sense of play and possibility that made time in Fred's classroom a joy for all of us, and it was the joy that allowed us to discover the most and best in ourselves. Facilitation at this level was simply being my most creative self while I offered what I knew to a teacher who used my knowledge and embellished it with his own creative impulses. Artists and teachers can form relationships where together they create something different, which is not the artist's nor the teacher's nor the student's, but is formed from the interests of all.

In another situation, Doran, a fourth grade teacher, told me that she loved to read. In hearing that, I suggested to her that we could make giant books with her students, whose reading skills were weak, where the children

could write a story together and illustrate it on large pieces of foam core. Because I was able to suggest a project that would expand on her interest and which would be wild enough to get the kid's attention, we all kept writing and illustrating longer than any of us thought possible.

Doran was able to articulate her interest to me, which sparked possibilities for how she could use her love of reading to create a project that she and the children would love, and would also fulfill her curriculum requirements. She may not have thought that she could express

her love of reading by making books with her students, and she certainly had not thought that unusual free materials, such as using five-feet sheets of foam core for the pages, might bring her and her students a uniquely rewarding way of doing language arts. Merely asking her about her interests modeled a different approach. Materializing it in the classroom further modeled that:

1) Free materials were available in the city;

2) A collaborative story could be written by the entire classroom;

3) This project did not have to take away from the precious "curriculum time", but WAS reading and writing;

4) The students could learn about the process of how books were made by exploring what it is to be an author, illustrator, and editor;

5) By following what you love, you can love what you do; and

6) Ideas emerge when you express your interests to another.

Toward a Model for Training Artists

A few artists in Chicago have learned an innovative model of facilitation, in which workshop participants learn from multiple approaches and discover not only a new way to teach, but a new way to learn. Much of the power of this approach is in the way we train.

Individually we study an artwork, but not in the usual

sense. Instead of collecting information by reading about an artist or artwork, we begin by using a three-step process: noticing, then interpreting, and finally creating an activity that will explore the perceived essence of the artwork. We then teach our activity to fellow artists, who help us reflect on its effect to reveal the meaning of the artwork before we present our workshops to teachers. The collaborative approach enhances our understanding of how to teach and gives us the same kind of experience that the teachers will have.

I have had the good fortune to be a member of a team of artists for the past six years offering one-, two-, and three-week intensive summer workshops for teachers. We have had the opportunity to continually question our goals and approaches to using this unique learning model. The hope is that, through continued support during the school year, through periodic seminars and classroom visits, that the transformative experience the teachers uniformly experience will ultimately reshape the way they teach. The program, the Chicago Arts Collaborative for Teachers (CACT), was inspired by the Lincoln Center Institute in New York and adapted to the resources we have in Chicago.

In order to make this model of facilitation clear, I will explain the process and applications to the curriculum. The process details a facilitation model that offers participants a method of acquiring experiences that enhance knowledge.

We were eight artists representing music, dance, drama, and visual arts. When we first gathered in the spring of 1993, we had only a general idea of how to prepare for teaching a process that would allow participants to experience a specific work of art, as well as the process

121

the artist used to create it. It would involve us becoming archeologists of sorts, detectives who would sleuth out what there was in specific artworks as though we had come to them for the first time without any preconceived ideas. We would create activities that would focus on an interpretation of the artwork, based on what we had noticed. That first summer showed us that this process was magical, an inside-out way of facilitation that brought "a-ha" experiences from the teachers. They got inside the works of art, unlike times when someone lectures "about" them. Without our talking about the artist, the work of art, or any of its particulars, the teachers personally encountered the essence of the artwork. Like peeling back an onion, they saw many layers of meaning.

It is thrilling when learning is approached this way. The activities we created were intended to present the teachers with simple questions that confronted the artist. Activities were structured so that groups of teachers were asked to probe and solve problems in the presence of their peers. They became more confident as they took risks, and found out that they could do more than they thought. Everyone broke through defenses and inhibitions and, as they did, the group bonded.

In the beginning, we unlearned how we usually taught, both the skills we all knew so well and our usual way of teaching them. Even though we were accomplished artists and teachers, we became immersed in a totally different and challenging approach of making knowledge known to others.

What do we do? We begin by simply noticing what is present in an artwork, observing its elements – eg. Color, shape, line, size, sound. This requires the nitty-gritty of continued looking and listening and looking and listening

some more. I remember standing in front of what looked
to me like an all black painting, entitled "Untitled", by
Clifford Still at the Art Institute in Chicago and wondering what all that blackness was about. I was uncomfort-
able not seeing anything specific. No content, not even
abstraction to focus on. However, as I continued to look, I
began to note texture and size and a tiny bit of red in the
lower left-hand corner. I became fascinated by what could
be expressed with so little. (In examining any artwork
this way, even when I think I know what the painting is
about, I hold off even mental interpretations and continue
noticing.)

I wondered what this painting was about, what the
artist was trying to say. I knew Still was an abstract
expressionist in the 50's who, along with other abstract
expressionists, rid themselves of the traditional rubrics of
painting in order to explore paint for its own sake. I
thought that this painting might be expressing silence, as
if the artist were inviting the viewer into an unknown
dark place to search for what is visible in the painting, a
symbol for searching within. By seeing all I could first
without interpreting, I was able to pause long enough to
create a space to continue looking for more information.
After I came to my own understanding of what this painting was about, I gathered more data, this time from
books: the dates, and the historical and cultural milieu
that shaped the work. This not only added to the information I had gathered by simply seeing, it affirmed the noticing and interpreting I had already done.

I created an activity that would probe the artwork's
essence. During the workshop with the teachers, I began
by turning off the lights in the windowless room we occu-
pied and asked how people felt in the dark. Do we, out of

123

our discomfort in dark places, seek familiar forms to make us feel safe? Could being in the dark also help us discover details that we might ordinarily miss if we could see everything? After observing our feelings of being in the dark and the sharpness of vision required to see forms, I gave everyone oil pastels and asked them to either work with one color, or to create one rich color by using several. They were to pay attention to texture. They could dig into the built-up layers of oil pastels with utensils or add wood-shavings with glue. I wanted the teachers to continue discovering what texture could reveal to them. I also asked them to introduce a surprise color. They worked for two hours!

Finally, we all went and stood in front of the Still painting. The teachers were able to be with this difficult painting in a very different way than if someone had lectured about it, the artist, the abstract expressionists, and then presented interpretations of what the consensus of critics thought the painting represented. In the way that we worked, the teachers were able to discover how this artist had worked, what he was after, and, by inference, what the movement of abstract expressionism and pure painting was about.

One of our goals is to give teachers tools with which to access an artwork. If the teaching artist thinks it is about color or story or contrast or mood or rhythm, he creates an activity that demonstrates those qualities. The surprise of not seeing or knowing about the artwork until after the activity is completed, allows participants to make connections between the activity and the artwork itself. It is in these moments that the "a-ha" of accessing many parts of knowing is deeply felt.

Reflection is an integral part of this process. Because

these experiences are so deeply felt, we make time to retrieve them and then to reflect on how to incorporate it into teaching. Writing helps validate and recover experiences. By making reflection part of the creative experience, we do what artists always do, critique their own work. By practicing remembering we come to understand its effect on how we create, both our lives and our curriculum.

This is a very powerful model of artist training. The artist first experiences what the teacher will be asked to experience. Both will have shared experience from which to draw out material to offer in the classroom.

The most important result of facilitating this way is that teachers experience a new way of being a learner and are transformed by their insights. To see normally inhibited teachers open up is a testament to this process. Having confidence allows teachers to approach curriculum in the same way they approached an artwork. We take any subject and, without a recipe for how to teach it, begin to explore, and again, to simply notice what is there. Approaching curriculum without the usual safe plan of how to teach it, we may acquire a new understanding of what the subject is about. We can then create an activity that will allow the students to understand from the inside out. The process is the same. The artwork is the curriculum. The teacher is now an artist.

Catalysts in the Classroom

Our job as art facilitators is to demonstrate another model, to point in another direction; to offer another way of approaching curriculum, another way to seeing students; to model another way of being. We engage teachers in their own creative expression. We are catalysts in the classroom. It takes courage and creativity to find a common ground that both artist and teacher can tread together, but when we do, there is a classroom full of naturally creative and eager students waiting for what we have to offer.

BIBLIOGRAPHY

Ashton-Warner, Sylvia. *Teacher*. New York: Simon and
  Schuster, Inc. 1963. Reprinted by Touchtone 1986.

Campbell, Joseph. *Myths to Live By*. Viking Press 1972.

Gardiner, Howard. *To Open Minds*. New York: Basic
  Books 1991.

Edwards, Carolyn; Gandini, Lella; Forman, George edi-
  tors. *The Hundred Languages of Children*. Ables
  Publishing 1993.

Gatto, John Taylor. "A Few Lessons They Won't Forget:
  The Disgrace of Modern Schooling." *The Sun* 1990: 4-8.

Graham, Patricia Albjerg. "Schools: Cacophony About
  Practice, Silence About Purpose." *Daedalus* 114 (Fall
  1984): 29-57.

Harris, Maria. *Teaching and Religious Imagination*. San
  Francisco: Harper & Row 1987.

Herndon, James. *How to Survive Your Native Land*. New
  York: Simon and Schuster 1971.

Nachmanovitch, Stephen. *Free Play*. Los Angeles: J.P.
  Tarcher Inc. 1990.

Symposium: Arts as Education, Part I and II, *Harvard
  Educational Review*, Vol. 61, No. 1, February 1991
  and Vol. 61, No. 3, August 1991.

Williams, William Carlos. *Autobiography*. New York:
  Random House 1948.

About The Author

Photo by: Jean Clough

Sue Sommers is an artist and educator. Her watercolors and painted cut-outs in wood have been exhibited in the midwest; Tucson, Arizona; and Oakland, California; as well as at an exhibition on Chicago at a museum in Jaipur, Rajasthan, India.

As an educator, she has worked as a facilitator and artist-in-residence primarily in the Chicago Public schools through arts and education organizations, grants, and universities. Her particular interest has been to foster the creative potential in teachers ever since she worked on a Ford Foundation grant in the 1970's.

She lives with her husband, Tor, in Evanston, IL.